The Burden of the Past

Studies in German Literature, Linguistics, and Culture

The Burden of the Past

Martin Walser on Modern German Identity
Texts, Contexts, Commentary

Thomas A. Kovach
and
Martin Walser

CAMDEN HOUSE
Rochester, New York

First published 2008
by Camden House

Camden House is an imprint of Boydell & Brewer Inc.
668 Mt. Hope Avenue, Rochester, NY 14620, USA
www.camden-house.com
and of Boydell & Brewer Limited
PO Box 9, Woodbridge, Suffolk IP12 3DF, UK
www.boydellandbrewer.com

ISBN-13: 978-1-57113-368-7
ISBN-10: 1-57113-368-2

Library of Congress Cataloging-in-Publication Data

Kovach, Thomas A., 1949
    The burden of the past : Martin Walser on modern German identity :
texts, contexts, commentary / Thomas A. Kovach.
        p. cm. — (Studies in German literature, linguistics, and culture)
Includes bibliographical references and index.
ISBN-13: 978-1-57113-368-7 (hardcover : alk. paper)
ISBN-10: 1-57113-368-2 (hardcover : alk. paper)
    1. Walser, Martin, 1927- — Political and social views. 2. Germany
— History — 1933-1945. I. Title. II. Series.

PT2685.A48Z74 2008
838'.91409—dc22

                                                                2008031161

A catalogue record for this title is available from the British Library.

This publication is printed on acid-free paper.
Printed in the United States of America.

For my daughter, Leah

Contents

Acknowlegments

I WOULD FIRST LIKE TO THANK my editor Jim Walker for his advice and support throughout this project — he has been a pleasure to work with at all times. I'd also like to think Sue Innes, the copy editor, whose very thorough and astute reading has helped with several difficult passages in the texts.

Then I'd like to thank Martin Walser himself for his helpful responses to several of my questions regarding the translations. Also, I'd like to thank his biographer Jörg Magenau for providing an extremely thoughtful and stimulating account of Walser's life and career, one that has greatly informed my commentaries.

I'd also like to thank my colleagues Albrecht Classen, Barbara Kosta, and Mary Wildner-Bassett for their helpful suggestions regarding some problematic passages in the translation of Walser's texts. I would like to thank the University of Arizona for granting me the sabbatical leave that enabled me to finish the project in timely fashion.

As always, I want to thank my wife Candy for her love, support, and patience with me.

And finally, I want to thank my daughter, Leah, to whom this volume is dedicated, for inspiring me with her wonderful musical and intellectual accomplishments.

Thomas Kovach
Tucson, Arizona
June 2008

The Burden of the Past

Introduction

ON OCTOBER 11, 1998, MARTIN WALSER, one of the most prominent of the postwar generation of German writers, gave a speech at
St. Paul's Church in Frankfurt am Main as he formally accepted the
"Peace Prize of the German Book Trade." This speech, which took place
in a historically weighty setting — the church had been the site of the
German National Assembly during the 1848 revolution, arguably the
first (albeit short-lived) democratic institution in German history —
addressed what Walser called the exploitation of the Holocaust, the use
of Holocaust remembrance by unnamed individuals to keep Germans in
a perpetual state of guilt. The speech was received by the assembled
notables with a standing ovation, with one significant exception: Ignatz
Bubis, the president of the Central Council of Jews in Germany, attacked
Walser in the press the next day for making incendiary comments designed (in Bubis's view) to stir up ultra-nationalist and antisemitic elements among the general public. This led to a rather ugly public debate
between Walser and Bubis, one that to this day remains a milestone in
the troubled history of Germany's struggle to come to terms with the
Nazi past. Despite Bubis's attempts to defuse the acrimony, finally even
withdrawing his comment about the incendiary nature of the speech, a
bitter aftertaste remained.

Shortly before his death in August of the following year, Bubis, who
had devoted much of his adult life to strengthening the position of the
Jewish community in Germany and insisting on the possibility of post-
Holocaust Jewish life in Germany, lamented in an interview that his life's
work had been in vain, and requested that he be buried in Israel.

In 2002, Walser published his novel *Tod eines Kritikers* (Death of a
Critic), in which the corrupt central character was a thinly veiled portrait
of the German-Jewish literary critic Marcel Reich-Ranicki; this led even
many of those who had defended him earlier (notably Frank Schirrmacher
of the leading daily, the *Frankfurter Allgemeine Zeitung*[1]) to attack him
for displaying an antisemitic agenda.

An outside observer might easily conclude that an apparently "respectable" postwar German author had been exposed as a closet Jew-

[1] Subsequently referred to as *FAZ.*

hater and/or right-winger, and this has indeed been the view taken by some in the years since. And yet, as Walser's defenders have pointed out, it is rather problematic to make such charges against a man who in the 1960s was noted for his left-wing political engagement (including a brief flirtation with the German Communist Party) and who, even more significantly, had taken the lead among German intellectuals in dealing not only with the Nazi past in general but specifically with the issue of the Holocaust; in his 1965 essay "Our Auschwitz," written in response to the Frankfurt Auschwitz trials, he spoke explicitly of collective German responsibility for the Holocaust and expressed his disdain for those who sought to evade this responsibility by focusing all the blame on the individuals on trial. How is it that the same person who in the 1960s seemed a model for his generation in dealing with the Holocaust and calling on his fellow Germans to acknowledge their share of responsibility for Nazi crimes, in the 1990s and since emerges as someone complaining about the burden imposed by Holocaust images and attacking the Berlin Holocaust Monument, then still under discussion, as a "nightmare"?

In the volume that follows I do not pretend to offer a definitive answer to this question. Rather, by presenting this and several other of Walser's speeches and essays dealing with issues of the German past in English translation, and by providing historical context and commentary on these texts, I hope to give readers a perspective from which they may begin to consider the issues that, as will become clear, concern not only Walser as an isolated figure but all of German society, East and West, in its ongoing struggle to deal with the Nazi past and its own conflicted feelings regarding that past.

*   *   *

Martin Walser was born in the town of Wasserburg, on Lake Constance in the south of Germany, in the year 1927. He himself was later to assert (in the essay "Handshake with Ghosts") that the fact of his being a German born in the year 1927 is more significant than any ideological orientation he may have displayed as a postwar intellectual. By this it may be assumed he meant that he was of the generation too young to bear any responsibility for the rise of Hitler or for crimes committed by the Nazi regime — he was a six-year-old child when Hitler came to power in 1933, and eighteen when the war ended in 1945 — but old enough to have witnessed, if only from the perspective of a provincial town, the realities of life under the Nazi regime, and to have served in the army as a young recruit. He thus entered adulthood under the shadow of his country's catastrophic defeat (in fact spending several months as an American POW at war's end), but, even more significantly, under the shadow of the postwar revelation of the horrors perpetrated by the German state.

After his release he completed his secondary-school studies and then began his university studies, first at the University of Regensburg, then (from 1948 onward) at the University of Tübingen, where he received his doctorate in 1952 with a dissertation on Franz Kafka. His choice of topic is worth noting, given the accusations of antisemitism that have been leveled at him in recent years, and the fact that in 1950 Kafka's place in the pantheon of major twentieth-century writers was nowhere near as secure as it is now. During Walser's student years he was heavily involved in student theater, and after his arrival in Tübingen he began working with the *Süddeutsche Rundfunk* (Southern German Radio[2]) in Stuttgart. His first literary efforts were in fact radio plays written to be broadcast over the SDR.

Walser was not involved at the start with the writers who formed the famous *Gruppe 47,* an organization of young German writers who set out to make a clean break with the Nazi past, favoring realistic prose anchored in the present. But he won the group's prize in 1955 with his short story "Templones Ende" and was henceforth associated with the group and some of its well-known members, such as Günter Grass and Heinrich Böll. In 1957 he published his first novel, *Ehen in Phillipsburg* (*Marriage in Phillipsburg,* 1961), for which he received the Hermann Hesse Award. The previous year he had left his job with the SDR in Stuttgart and returned with his wife to the Lake Constance region, where he has lived ever since. At the same time he traveled widely, notably making several trips to the United States, the first in 1958 to participate in the Harvard International Seminar at the invitation of Henry Kissinger. His 1960 novel *Halbzeit* (*Half Time*), the first of the so-called Anselm Kristlein trilogy and still regarded as one of his major works, brought him greater renown. However, his primary focus in these early years remained the drama. Interestingly, his 1964 play *Der schwarze Schwan* (*The Black Swan*) is widely regarded as one of the first literary texts by a German author to deal with issues of German national guilt for crimes of the Nazi era; its young protagonist is driven to suicide by his discovery of his father's involvement in wartime atrocities.

[2] Subsequently referred to as SDR.

Our Auschwitz (1965)

Context

DURING THE FIRST DECADES FOLLOWING THE WAR, West German society was preoccupied with the task of rebuilding its physical structure after the damage caused by Allied bombardment of German cities and creating a vibrant new economy — an accomplishment widely known as the "Wirtschaftswunder" or Economic Miracle. Most Germans wanted above all to put the past behind them, a desire (as argued by Alexander and Margarethe Mitscherlich in their 1967 book *Die Unfähigkeit zu trauern* [*The Inability to Mourn*][1]) that sometimes verged on a kind of pathological denial, even a tendency to think of themselves as the real victims. The writers of *Gruppe 47* were an exception, in that they did address issues stemming from the Nazi past, including the complicity of "ordinary Germans" in Hitler's rise to power. But even they, as Ernestine Schlant argued in her more recent book *The Language of Silence: West German Literature and the Holocaust* (1999),[2] were notably silent regarding what most people today regard as the most horrendous and lasting element of that past — the Holocaust.

The postwar Nuremberg trials, which brought some of the top Nazi leaders to trial, did much to document and expose the details of the atrocities committed under the regime, but the fact that these trials were initiated and conducted by the victorious allies (neither West nor East Germany had yet been established) led many Germans to dismiss them as "victors' justice." By contrast, the so-called Auschwitz Trials, which took place in Frankfurt am Main in the early 1960s, were conducted entirely

---

[1] Alexander Mitscherlich and Margarethe Mitscherlich, *The Inability to Mourn: Principles of Collective Behavior*, trans. Beverly R. Placzek (New York: Grove Press, 1975).

[2] Ernestine Schlant, *The Language of Silence: West German Literature and the Holocaust* (New York: Routledge, 1999).

under the auspices of the Federal Republic of Germany (West Germany), and thus arguably had a greater impact on the consciousness of most Germans. This was the case even though those who were put on trial were lower functionaries in the administration of the death camp, since the Commandant Rudolf Höss and other senior officials had been turned over to Poland and put on trial in 1947.

Among the many in attendance at some of the trials was Martin Walser, who by the 1960s had a well-established reputation as a writer, and who was also known for his strong left-wing political engagement, in association with the SPD or Social Democratic Party. The following essay first appeared in 1965. The names he mentions — Kaduk, Boger, Sorge, Schubert, Broad, Hofmann, Baretzki, Capesius, Stark, Klehr, Bednarik — are those of some of the more notorious defendants.

Martin Walser: Our Auschwitz (1965)

If you want to make a nice life for yourself,
You must not worry about what is past.
— Goethe, *"Rules of Life"*

1.

THE TRIAL OF THE AUSCHWITZ FUNCTIONARIES has taken on an importance that has nothing to do with the legal business involved. Historical research is part of it, but also revelations, and the moral and political education of a population that clearly could not be brought by any other means to recognize what had happened.

For more than a year now we've been reading in the newspapers what went on in Auschwitz. Perhaps we were even present at the courtroom in Frankfurt. We know the faces of the accused, we remember individual witnesses, and above all we remember the frightful details. The unbelievable has imprinted itself most deeply into our consciousness. The unimaginable has made the most lasting impression. Everyone now knows the horrible instruments of torture and death and can quote individual words from the jargon of the perpetrators and from the language of the victims; everyone knows certain buildings and locations in Auschwitz and the murderous rituals practiced there; people imagine the removal of corpses, the bodies abused and tortured in one way or another. For over a year we've read captions like the following: "Women thrown alive into the fire," "Soup and street droppings stuffed into the mouths of inmates," "Deathly ill inmates chewed on by rats," "Chicken and vanilla ice cream for the executioners," "Finishing off inmates with a shot during the morning break," "The victims in the gas chamber screamed for almost 15 minutes," "Alcohol flowed in Auschwitz," "Shot in the head by the black wall," "A devil sits in the dock," "Like birds of prey."

Kaduk and Boger are the ones whose pictures the newspapers especially like to show. They've become stars. Reduced to the dimensions of a quote. They are the epitome of Auschwitz. The more horrible the individual event, the more precisely it was communicated. The more unfathomable the detail, the more clearly it was described to us.

So our memory is now filled with frightful material. And automatically, the more frightful the Auschwitz quotations are, the clearer our distance from Auschwitz becomes. We have nothing to do with these events, with these horrors — this we know for a fact. These acts of brutality can't be shared. This trial isn't about us. It's not for nothing that the accused are called "devils" and "executioners" and "beasts of prey" in the news reports. After all, who among us is a devil, an executioner, a beast of prey? Actually, once such distance has been established, it's possible to observe Auschwitz. In fact, Auschwitz manages to exert a sad kind of attraction. Reports about the crimes committed in Auschwitz end up in the vicinity of reports about other crimes: "Seventeen bite marks and head injuries," "They went to their deaths singing," "Death by starvation lasted fifteen days."

The fascination that what is horrible exerts on us is well known. And it's through this that Auschwitz is attaining historical prominence among us, if it is at all. As a quotation about horrors. That's just the way we are. No one, I believe, could watch what was going on in the Frankfurt courtroom regularly without being both repulsed and attracted by these quotations. The question is: are people conscious of the nature of this fascination? Again and again the word "inferno" appears in the newspaper reports. Dante is being evoked. One of the editors of the documents from the trials of SS officials in Buchenwald and Sachsenhausen wrote: "Perhaps the imagination of a Dante, who depicted the torments of hell, could have conceived of the reality of the crimes committed in the concentration camps." Now, once again, the name of Dante keeps popping up in reports of the Auschwitz trial. People talk about "Dantesque scenes."

Perhaps the reporters want to escape the pure brutality of the headline, and in the process of doing so they enter a context even more alien to the reality of Auschwitz than the daily news reports of robberies, murders, and sex killings. To compare Auschwitz with Dante's Inferno is almost a kind of insolence, unless one can plead ignorance. After all, in Dante's Inferno, sinners were atoning for their sins. And in any case, after the Inferno came the Purgatorio and Paradiso. If the prisoners of Auschwitz had been cruelly asked by a visitor named Dante to recite the sins for which they were being punished, they would have been at a loss to reply. And their torment was followed only by their extermination.

But what is the source of the tendency to call the SS functionaries "devils" and "beasts" and to circumscribe the torments of real human beings by calling on Dante, and thus to make a "hell" out of Auschwitz? There's no question: it's because for the reporters Auschwitz is simply not a reality. Anyone watching the trial can tell right away that Auschwitz is something real only for the "inmates"[3] who survived. The SS functionaries describe their activities as the requirements of their defense strategy dictate. That's their right. Still, one doesn't easily concede that it's so easy for them to stay in the jargon of their routine activities. And one doesn't know yet for sure whether they use this jargon because within in it any notion of individual responsibility is practically nonexistent, or whether they don't have any authentic language for their memory of Auschwitz.

Only the "inmates" know what Auschwitz was. No one else. When a former "prisoner" in the courtroom is unable to speak any more, when he has difficulty even looking at his former torturers in order to identify one of them, when, as if under some compulsion, he repeats the turns of phrase of his torturers, twenty-year-old sentences, even the sentences of those being tortured, when for a couple of minutes memory delivers its bad matter simply and without amplification, then something of Auschwitz becomes real. The witness Johann Wrobel said in the trial of the Sachsenhausen officers: "When I saw Sorge and Schubert again on TV, I had to cry." It is due not to the guilt of the SS functionaries but simply to the nature of our human memory that these SS functionaries don't have to cry when they now see the former "inmates." Our memory labors onward, in a manner that is difficult to perceive, trying to process our experiences, which it takes in, but when we remember a situation, then our memory provides us first of all with an image of our role in the situation at the time when it occurred. Then, as we know from recent insights, we can manipulate our role, we can regret it, deny it, recant it. But these commentaries, which we now assign to the content of our memory, cannot really achieve any power over us. That's why we shouldn't be too surprised that the defendants often smile or give answers that sound almost ironic. That's not cynicism. Even today they can't grasp the reality of the Auschwitz "inmates," because their memory has preserved an entirely different Auschwitz; their own Auschwitz, that of the SS functionaries.

But Auschwitz has become important because of the "inmates"; what was done to the "inmates" is the content of the trial and is our national difficulty. And it is precisely this reality of the concentration camp about which we know even less than we do about that of the SS functionaries. This situation of absolute lawlessness is absolutely unimaginable to us.

---

[3] Here and throughout the rest of the essay, Walser places quotation marks around this word ("Häftlinge"), as if to signal that the ordinary word for the inmate of a prison is grotesquely inappropriate to describe Holocaust victims.

Thus, since we can't really understand the situation of the "inmates," because the degree of their suffering surpasses every previous measure, and because as a result we cannot create any human image of the immediate perpetrators, Auschwitz is called a hell and perpetrators are devils. In this way one could explain why words like this, which point outside our world, are used whenever there is talk of Auschwitz.

But Auschwitz was not hell; it was a German concentration camp. And the "inmates" were not damned or half-damned souls in a Christian cosmos, but innocent Jews, Communists, and so forth. And the torturers were not fantastic devils, but people like you and me: Germans, or those who wanted to become Germans.

Our lack of experience and the boundlessness of the crimes committed are without doubt one reason for the fact that we try to keep Auschwitz at arm's length by using this kind of language. We simply capitulate in the face of so much "inhumanity." Then we collect quotations based on how much brutality can be perceived in them. The conditions that allowed for this brutality are far too colorless, too completely situated in the realm of the historical, the political, the social, so they fade away in the face of the juicy embodiment of an SS man whom we stylize as a devil. We care just as little about the conditions when we read Dante. We detach the pure horrors from their context and make Dante into a master of brutality; thus we can use him in describing the horrors of Auschwitz, which also appear to us as horrors in and of themselves, as pure brutality. But even if we plunder and falsify Dante and the Christian conception of hell purely for the sake of effect, we should still be a bit more careful when it comes to Auschwitz. Here the circumstances play far too great a role; in this case it is precisely the circumstances that made it possible for Auschwitz to arise among us. We will never understand how Auschwitz was for the "inmates." But what made it possible for there to be an Auschwitz for these "inmates" shouldn't get lost in a flight into fantastic circumlocutions — half tabloid, half Dante.

Auschwitz is not something fantastic, but rather an institution that the German state created, with great care and planning, for the exploitation and extermination of human beings. When we, with pleasure masked by self-pity (which can also express itself as a national protest), learn of the brutal facts in the newspaper, we easily forget that all these colorful medieval-style tortures were instituted rather against the system. Our Nazis were just getting started. Personal cruelty would sooner or later not have been allowed to play a role. The former "inmate" Dr. Wolken called the gruesome practices of the SS functionaries "busy work." One forgets, in face of the memorable torturers of Auschwitz, that they were worse idealists than the better idealists who had designed the system. Truly, it was to become, as Ossietzky observed, "the time of the disinfected torturer's stake."

One must imagine the death factory without the props and attributes with which the defendants are now being reproached: without Kaduk's hiking cane, without Boger's swing, without Broad's wish to shoot the prettier women first, without Hofmann's "sport," without Baretzki's deadly "special blow" with the edge of his hand, without Stark's political zeal directed against Soviet commissars, without Capesius's vulnerability to certain items of value, without Klehr's addiction to playing the role of a doctor, without Bednarik's desire to kill people with a chair, without shovel handles, without whips made from bulls or water hoses. . . . Auschwitz without these "colors" is the real Auschwitz. Selection at the ramp, transport to the gas chambers, Zyklon B, crematoria. And: whoever isn't murdered works for Krupp or IG Farben until he dies or is murdered. That's the operating system. That's how it was developed by the idealists of National Socialism. As part of a greater system. The personal satisfactions of the functionaries were opposed and would certainly have been suppressed completely in a time of ill-fated peace.

There was much more to be learned about the so-called Third Reich in the Nuremberg trials than there was in the Auschwitz trial. Nevertheless, the effect of those trials on all of us was rather slight. That cannot only be because we didn't want our leaders to be judged by foreign tribunals. Perhaps it was also because we still have no sense for the asocial element that appears in a nicely bourgeois manner and legitimizes itself before acting. The content of the Nuremberg trials was obviously not fit for popularization. Nevertheless, in those trials the attempt was made to trace the historical events back to the actions and decisions of individuals and organizations and to determine their responsibility. In the Auschwitz trials, only functionaries sat in the dock. Henchmen, executioners, people who had been seduced, products of a German education in violence. Perpetrators in the most old-fashioned sense of the word. And if they were devils, then rather poor devils. The lower the functionary, the more he was dependent on a tangible deed. And the more tangible the deed, the easier it was to free it from the conditions of the system, from our German history between 1918 and 1945. And this process of unhinging the deed from our national context as a personal crime continues until nothing remains except pure brutality.

One hears a fascinating quote, takes it in while shuddering, willingly and unwillingly at the same time, and still thinks: I'm not like them. But which of us does not surrender to the fascination, these warring emotions we feel when faced with the pure and thus sparkling brutality of these figures, whom we stylize until they become devils and beasts of prey! Of course we despise the perpetrators. That's part of our intimate inner debate. We sense the difference. And we commiserate with the victims. The pain of the victims, this torment borrowed from Dante's vocabulary, this part of the quotation is absolutely essential for our experience. Only through the pathetic attempt to place ourselves on the side of the victims, or at least to imagine as best we can how horrible their suffering was — only through this commiseration does the perpetrator become as despicable and brutal as we need him to be to justify our sentiment, a sentiment that is lacking in reality but at the moment quite intense.

After a few moments of rest and reflection, we can of course see that we won't succeed in sharing in the pain of the victims. What does that even mean, we share in their pain? What is our regret worth? Does it help us to do anything? It is even possible that our interest in the victims is less than our interest in the cruelties to which they were subjected. How long will we carry the Auschwitz quotations around with us? I believe that we will quickly forget Auschwitz once again if we come to know it only as a collection of subjective brutalities. Why do we forget the daily murders and sex killings as soon as the criminals have disappeared behind bars? Perhaps it's because in the reports about these cases the factual element was the most important thing. It's said that this has a lasting effect on the unconscious, for instance among youths. Whether it was done with a hammer, how it happened, how often, whether it was in the kitchen or on a dock — these are the questions that take center stage. We absorb the information with feelings that tug in this and that direction, more for its entertainment value than critically, and then we forget it once more, and the next day we take in the next murder in the papers. Rarely does our insight into the circumstances that condition such deeds increase from one murder to the next. The richness of detail in the reports, and the brutality contained therein, put a stop to any reflection. Our consciousness remains empty. And since neither Höss nor Heydrich nor Himmler nor any racial ideologue or IG Farben executive is sitting in the dock, it is even conceivable that the Auschwitz trial would become for us a monstrous and tangled mass of sensationalist murder trials, and our only involvement with it would be as the consumers of lurid headlines. And those get forgotten as soon as they are replaced by new headlines.

Who still remembers what it was like in Buchenwald and Sachsen-hausen? The trials of Sommer, the "hangman of Buchenwald," of "Iron Gustav" and "Pistol Schubert," were documentations of horrendous subjective cruelties. In a case like this, any comparison is excluded. And we were informed of the horrible inspirations of the defendants. Did these brutalities really reach our consciousness? Did they teach us what fascism is? Have we been able to force open that intricate connection between fascism and hyper-Germanness that survived the war (and not only in the heads of those from Lower Saxony)? Have we perhaps become more political in our relations with Eastern Europe, that is, more reasonable and modest in our demands? Do we have a somewhat better understanding of how deeply ingrained their fear of us must be after our last performance? Have we become more careful with respect to our idealistic talent, which always seduces us into building up worldviews like dungeons for ourselves and for those whom we stylize into ideal enemies — until we (and our enemies) behave just as enemies are supposed to behave? The impulse that came to fruition in Auschwitz had its origins long ago, and it had bad parents. Jews and Slavs — we'd been drilled about them in school for a long time. Now we're being reeducated to focus on Communists instead.

2.

If the concentration camp trials are supposed to be proof, as it's claimed, that we do not shy away from "dealing" with our past, they should have some sort of political repercussions. The fact that the trials are taking place at all is required by penal law and thus no proof of greater political openness. But Sorge, Sommer, Schubert, and their other Auschwitz colleagues can be presented to us by the prosecutors only in their subjective deeds, and these are such that our sense of distance is not threatened for a moment. We lived in a different state, so to speak, than the accused from 1933 to 1945.

In the bill of indictment for the Auschwitz trials, the prosecutors provided a thorough foundation for all the charges brought against the defendants. They placed the perpetrators and their deeds firmly within the reality of the so-called Third Reich. But in the trial itself and in the news reports about the trial, the only time that the reality of this "Reich," which affected all of us, was addressed was when the experts, the historians, gave their testimony. This is understandable, because after all the trial can address only the deeds for which perpetrators can be found. But the fact that until some point in time between 1918 and

1945 these perpetrators could have been confused with any of us, and that after that point due to special circumstances they followed the path that led them to this trial — this fact cannot be expressed adequately in such a trial. There is talk in the trial of deeds we would not have committed — either because we actually belong to those who enable deeds without actually performing them, or because during the time that the enabling of these deeds was occurring we were too young, or cunning enough to keep ourselves at a beneficial distance.

There's also no doubt that we Germans had no idea these brutalities were taking place. This too is an effect of this process. We are no longer under suspicion as accessories to the crime. In the face of these brutalities, which were systematically prepared but then carried out in glaring subjectivity, we lose the last remnant of solidarity with these perpetrators. We forget, numbed so to speak by the outcome, that we were at the very least patient witnesses while from 1933 to 1945 one step after another took place before our eyes: from the "Decree for the Protection of *Volk*[4] and State" of February 28, 1933, to the "Law for the Restoration of the Professional Civil Service" of April 7, 1933, to the "Law for the Protection of German Blood and German Honor" of September 15, 1935, to the decrees that made *Kristallnacht* possible, and also the decrees of November of 1938 that achieved their final goal in the "Thirteenth Decree Governing Citizenship in the Reich," which handed over our Jewish citizens once and for all to the arbitrary control of the SS. Even if we had had some feeling that we were too patient observers of this development, now we say to ourselves quite emphatically: we didn't know anything.

And in fact, the monstrous reality of Auschwitz may well exceed the powers of imagination of the citizen who patiently watches while Jews and Communists disappear from his neighborhood. On other hand, it would be disastrous if the monstrousness of the Auschwitz trial material led us to the point where in the future we viewed the so-called Third Reich only from the same distance from which we perceive the horrors of Auschwitz. Unfortunately, one must guess that we were closer to that state than we want to admit when face-to-face with its manifestation in Auschwitz.

---

[4] I have left the word *Volk* untranslated throughout these essays, for several reasons. First, it is a word familiar to English speakers. Second, there is no precise equivalent in English; neither "folk" nor "people" nor "nation" precisely captures the flavor of the German word. Finally, especially in the later essays, Walser tends to use the word as a kind of provocation, with full awareness of its association with Nazi discourse.

Or does Auschwitz not concern me at all? If something German erupted at Auschwitz, what is the German element in me that erupted there? I don't perceive my share in Auschwitz, that's for sure. So at the point where feelings of shame ought to arise, where conscience ought to be heard, I'm not affected. To be sure, I always have a hard time digging up what is German in myself. (I can only hope that other Germans, when they consider the matter precisely enough, also have their problems with this.) And in spite of this, I'm supposed to see myself vis-à-vis Auschwitz implicated in the crimes of the German people.

Idealistic thought-artists, both within and outside Germany, have helpfully shown since 1945 that there is no such thing as collective guilt. This proof is no hardship for an idealist. He loves to elevate his concept of personal responsibility to as high a position as possible. He wants to be able to expect something from people. From a single person. From an individual. This indivisible element has free will, the idealist discovers or decrees. It doesn't matter to him how much such an individual is composed of biological or political history. Nor does the experience of our idealists from 1918 until today matter, an experience that shows what grotesquely different stances this indivisible individual can assume in quick succession (and even simultaneously). In any case: since 1945 and in view of the Auschwitz trial this idealistic loophole has come in handy for us. Since each individual is responsible for himself, each one must take responsibility for his actions and his alone. If someone was guilty, that's his business.

And each of us easily confirms this for himself through his feeling of complete innocence when he hears something about Auschwitz. But perhaps this comes rather from the fact that his own belonging to the ethnic or national collective really can't be felt. Anyone who reflected on the deliberate and (even more) the involuntary share any individual has in the actions of the collective, instead of exploring his clear conscience and questioning his feeling of shame, could not so easily say: the deeds concern only those who did the deeds. If we chose the terms for our human nature a bit more carefully, making them more fitting, and therefore more realistic, then the causes would be as important as the results.[5] Then someone who makes a great murderer out of a little fellow is just as responsible as the one who carries out the murder. And the one who merely made a good deal of money from the murder and now once again is tinkering with corporate groups or is in charge of factories, he would

---

[5] There is a play on words in the German that cannot be reproduced: the German terms are "Ursache" (= cause, literally "original thing") vs. "Sache" (= thing).

be publicly assigned his share in mass murder. But the idealistic penal law prefers to look at the hands that perform actions. And those of the political or economic parties responsible don't show any blood. That's good bourgeois justice. The further down the ladder a person was, the worse off he is. There's no collective guilt. And we prefer not to speak of a collective cause.

How close this bourgeois individualist comes to anarchism! Why do we still speak of *Volk* or state at all, when in a difficult situation I can call on my personal feeling of innocence? I know already that my feeling of shame or my conscience does not reach as far as matters of state or *Volk*. And what is German in me probably gets noticed only by a foreigner. But I can reflect on the question of in what way and to what extent I belong to the West German state today, and also the question of in what way and to what extent the so-called Third Reich was entitled to manifest itself as the expression of my statehood. My citizenship is concrete. One can't get to the bottom of the question of citizenship through feeling, but at most through a kind of thinking.

The idealist is content to stay with the thought that he shares his nationality with Goethe, Kant, and Hegel (perhaps with Marx as well). But he has nothing in common with Goebbels, Göring, Heydrich, and Himmler (though perhaps something with Ludendorff). But if state and *Volk* are still meaningful designations for something political, thus for a collective that emerges historically and in the name of which laws are ordained or broken, then everything that happens is determined by this collective, and then the cause of everything must be sought in this collective. Then no deed can be purely subjective any more. Then Auschwitz is a collective German phenomenon. Then everyone is to some extent part of the cause of Auschwitz. Then it would be the task of each individual to discover his share of responsibility. One need not have been a member of the SS.

If we observe ourselves and others in the encounter with the Auschwitz trial, then we learn that as an exemplary trial of socially conditioned asocial behavior it mobilizes in textbook fashion our own idealistic and asocial inheritance: our share in Auschwitz.

The pathetic nationalistic protests against the trial are easily revealed as the most stupid way imaginable of caring for the reputation of the fatherland as a German idealist (or fascist). But our distance from the SS functionaries is also idealistic in the saddest way. We're not like them! But at the same time we find the punishment awaiting these SS functionaries ridiculously inappropriate, when we consider the horrendous "busy work" they performed in Auschwitz. Apparently we still think that a deed can be atoned for. And now this deed called Auschwitz, which exceeds every previous concept! But probably we simply want to be left alone. Punishment, end of story. If the perpetrators were treated at least to some extent as they treated others, we would probably feel better. Thus do the SS functionaries draw us into their idealistic way of thinking and acting. Thus one is drawn into the wake of the asocial. Thus do we capitulate before the effort to leave the asocial instinct behind us without satisfactory resolution. We want our peace. And it has the beautiful name of justice. The fact that for such deeds there can be no clearing of the deck, no atonement, is unpleasant for us.

We want to escape this history. And the justice system is supposed to help us achieve this. And what do we do with the sufferings of the "inmates"? Since we cannot succeed in creating any kind of meaning for them that could satisfy us, our instinct takes refuge once more in the idea of retribution. As if this vast quantity of suffering would then be somewhat less meaningless. We shy away from the effort of taking Auschwitz into our consciousness as a senseless murder that can never be atoned for. We cling to the subjective brutalities. They attract us and repel us. We allow ourselves to be attracted and repelled. We isolate the brutalities, but we are bored by the causes. Our well-established distance from the "devils" and "beasts" allows us to consume the glaring quotations as fodder for our own asocial nature, which we keep hidden. We can allow ourselves to do this all the more easily, since we bring to the victims our entire powerless sense of regret. And the justice system will fulfill its social task, after all, and take care of the matter legally.

That's the way it is, because that's the way we are. Among human beings, the talent for the social, which the idealist calls the humane, is still so weak, and the asocial so strong, that the perpetrators couldn't learn any more, and neither could those who belong to the side of the perpetrators. Only the victims, if they're still barely alive, and those who stand on the side of the victims, are unable to forget Auschwitz or to live on as if Auschwitz had never happened. But for us Auschwitz will have no consequences. The primitive politician has his anticommunism or his atom bomb or his support for the death penalty; the sensitive spirit is similarly served by his subtle relationship to cruelty. Our asociality still has its vulgar and refined functionaries; however much it may conceal itself at the moment, it can be mobilized at any time. Of course Auschwitz will never be repeated. The next triumph of the asocial will have different props. That's why it's so senseless and satisfying to perceive Auschwitz only in its one-time facts and so to speak only through one's nerves. But please — we're a successful society right now. And success makes one insensitive. Our consciousness feels no need. But our nerves need heavy doses. It's possible that toward the end of the century we will again be as bored as were the finer individuals at the beginning of the century. Finally we'll come up with some ideas. And that can easily be the beginning of the horror.

Commentary

IT IS NOT DIFFICULT TO SEE why those who defended Walser following his controversial 1998 speech cited this essay more than any other
to refute the charge that he was opposing Holocaust remembrance. It is
cited also by others whose interest is not in defending Walser but in
examining the legal and moral issues raised in the prosecution of those
who perpetrated war crimes and other atrocities, for instance a recent
article by Rebecca Wittmann.[6] Especially considering the fact that even
the politically engaged writers who were Walser's colleagues tended to
avoid the subject, to say nothing of the masses of ordinary Germans, it
can scarcely be denied that Walser deserves credit for his forceful engagement with the topic.

What is most striking is that although he in no way opposes the trials
being carried out — he speaks of his fellow Germans at the very beginning as "a population that clearly could not be brought by any other
means to recognize what had happened" — he is most critical of how the
proceedings are presented in the media, and how, largely as a result of
that presentation, the average German takes in these reports. He argues
that all aspects of this presentation — the obsession with gory details, the
attention to the particularly sadistic actions of the defendants, and the
tendency to describe it all with terms like "infernal" and "Dantesque" —
serve in fact to distance Germans from the proceedings. The extreme
nature of the individuals and their actions in fact allows average German
readers to reassure themselves that they have nothing to do with and
nothing in common with these monsters: "We're not like them!" At the
same time, he suggests that the media's extensive presentation of gruesome details is both a response to and an incitement of the public's hidden fascination with these morbid elements.

What is wrong, one might ask at first, with calling these imagined
scenes from Auschwitz "infernal" or "Dantesque"? Walser's reply:
"Auschwitz was not hell, but rather a German concentration camp. . . ."
In other words, these descriptive adjectives, however unobjectionable
they may seem at first glance, in fact serve to deflect the viewer's
attention from the reality that this was not a horrific scene of the afterlife
involving souls who had (according to Dante) merited eternal damnation
but something that took place in this world, and that was instigated by

---

[6] "Torture on Trial: Prosecuting Sadists and the Obfuscation of Systematic Crime,"
South Central Review 24:1 (Spring 2007): 8–17.

the German state. The attention to horrific details also tends to distract attention from the greater horror: the reality of the system that designed this machinery of murder.

The essay touches on one of the most hotly debated questions that arose especially in response to the revelation of the Holocaust, but that also pertains to other acts of genocide or other atrocities carried out by a state: can one speak of collective guilt or responsibility, or do such concepts apply only at the individual level? Obviously, most Germans of the postwar period chose to limit the notions of guilt and responsibility to those directly implicated in perpetrating the Holocaust or war crimes. This view was shared by others who were in no way implicated in war crimes, for instance, the American essayist Dwight MacDonald.[7] The question of guilt presupposes some knowledge of the crimes committed, and on this question Walser takes a very discerning position, on the one hand acknowledging that the average German had no knowledge of the specific horrors perpetrated at Auschwitz and other camps, but at the same time refuting the claim "we knew nothing" by enumerating the publicly announced laws and decrees that made the Holocaust possible, and of which Germans were fully informed.

But he speaks most directly to the issue of collective responsibility in the passage toward the end of the essay in which he writes:

> If state and *Volk* are still meaningful designations for something political, thus for a collective that emerges historically and in the name of which laws are ordained or broken, then everything that happens is determined by this collective, then the cause of everything must be sought in this collective. Then no deed can be purely subjective any more. Then Auschwitz is a collective German phenomenon. Then everyone is to some extent part of the cause of Auschwitz. Then it would be the task of each individual to discover his share of responsibility. One need not have been a member of the SS.

Here he states plainly that every German is implicated to some degree in the crimes committed, and that all should search their conscience to determine their share of responsibility. Thus there is no question that Walser in the mid-1960s was in the forefront of public voices in West Germany insisting on a collective German responsibility for the Holocaust, and consequently on the necessity for Germans to be aware of and reflect on the horrors committed and their causes.

This is not to say, however, that the essay is totally unproblematic. To begin with what may appear to be a minor stylistic point, in the

[7] Dwight Macdonald, "The Responsibility of Peoples," *Politics* 2 (Mar. 1945): 86–87.

paragraph quoted from above, in which he points out that Auschwitz was not hell but rather a German concentration camp, he goes on to say that its victims were not damned souls but "Jews, Communists, and so forth." Some might question the lumping together of those who were deported because they were political enemies of the regime (Communists) with those whose deportation was based solely on their "race" or ethnicity (Jews). Beyond this, the phrase "and so forth" seems a bit callous; it might be read as displaying a lack of empathy with the victims. This suspicion is confirmed by a statement that may at first glance seem one of exemplary honesty: "We will never understand how Auschwitz was for the 'inmates.'" Of course it is reasonable to state that no one who was not an inmate of Auschwitz can ever fully grasp what it was like to be there. But Walser seems to insist on a wall of separation between victim and perpetrator, and by extension between the contemporaries and descendents of victims and perpetrators respectively. Later he even speaks scornfully of "the pathetic attempt to place ourselves on the side of the victim," as if even the attempt to empathize is ridiculous.

This last point does not invalidate the forthrightness and courage that Walser displayed in writing this essay, but it does indicate at least one problematic area that will become increasingly apparent in the following essays.

His critique of how the brutal details of Auschwitz are presented in the media might also be linked with his later confessions of "looking away" from Holocaust images in the media; Jörg Magenau argues that his unapologetic statement in the Peace Prize speech about looking away from these images implies not an intention to forget the past but merely a protest against the way in which this past is commonly presented: that is, through horrific images.[8]

Finally, given the concern with German national identity that will play a major role in the texts that follow, it is interesting to note that even in this 1965 essay he comments: "I always have a hard time digging up what is German in myself" and later: "What is German in me probably gets noticed only by a foreigner." Both these comments point to his awareness even in the 1960s of the problem that postwar Germans tend to avoid any acknowledgment or even awareness of their national identity, preferring to identify either as Europeans or with the West or East German state.

---

[8] Jörg Magenau, *Martin Walser: Eine Biographie* (Reinbek bei Hamburg: Rowohlt, 2005), 487.

No End to Auschwitz (1979)

Context

IN 1965, WHEN WALSER WROTE HIS ESSAY "Our Auschwitz," he was becoming increasingly involved in politics, initially through the Social Democratic Party (SPD). Then, when he and other left-wing intellectuals grew increasingly frustrated in the late 1960s with the German government's cooperation with the US war effort in Vietnam and the SPD's failure to offer effective opposition to this policy, he became associated with the "Extra-Parliamentary Opposition" (APO) and even flirted with the German Communist Party. This development was given further impetus by the "Grand Coalition" of 1966 to 1969, in which the Social Democrats (led by Willy Brandt) joined in a coalition with the Christian Democrats, under the leadership of Kurt Kiesinger, the West German Chancellor, who had been a member of the Nazi Party. Ironically, given that his political engagement around this time took the form of opposition to American policies, it is widely thought that it was his sojourn in the United States in the late 1950s that brought him out of his relatively apolitical stance of the 1950s and convinced him of his obligation as a writer and public intellectual to speak out on political issues. The stance he adopted in the 1965 essay can be viewed as symptomatic of his assuming the role of a public intellectual commenting on political and moral issues of concern to his society. His left-wing political outlook was reflected in his novels and plays during these years, which often featured individuals whose lives were controlled in destructive ways by the ruling economic and political power structure.

In the mid-1970s, disillusioned by his frustrating experiences with the Communist Party, and with the Vietnam War over, he withdrew for the most part from his political engagement of the preceding years. In spite of his bitter opposition to the Vietnam War, Walser maintained a strong sympathy for the United States, which was reflected and reinforced by his repeated visits as guest professor at several American colleges and universities: Middlebury College in Vermont and the University of Texas (1973), West Virginia University (1976), Dartmouth College in New Hampshire (1979), and the University of California at Berkeley (1983).

In 1979 Walser received an invitation to speak at the opening of an exhibition of drawings by Auschwitz inmates. What follows is the text of that speech.

Martin Walser: No End to Auschwitz (1979)

NOT A SINGLE DAY HAS PASSED since Auschwitz. There is a way of measuring time in which one need not calculate whether or not crimes have passed the statute of limitations.[1] This is the time measurement called history. The fact that in this measurement of time not a day has passed since Auschwitz can be perceived in every encounter with the reality of Auschwitz. We cannot speak about Auschwitz with the historical detachment with which we speak of genocides that occurred in the nineteenth century. A single image from a concentration camp, and we have nothing more to say. Or would someone be so bold as to explain to us how we, how our people, came to do such things? It is only too understandable that survivors and the families of victims are striving for justice through punishment; it is also understandable that we who belong to the community of the perpetrators believe we can unburden ourselves by seeking punishment for them. I personally do not share this belief. From the individual stories of perpetrators we know that nothing is so important to them as the explanation of their deed. They must become understandable to themselves. They have to know why they have done something. And this "why" then contains in itself a kind of justification. It is impossible for the individual to bear pure guilt. And for a people, a society? In any case, we help ourselves to deal with this by shifting the guilt, the concretely frightful element, onto a handful of those who just followed orders. But we cannot avoid the responsibility of answering the question as to how, among our nation of well-educated citizens, there suddenly were a few who were capable of such things. There cannot be any academic field or group of fields that could make what happened comprehensible through a cause-and-effect relationship. There are no causes that were designed to produce such effects. And yet this murder factory arose through us. It was developed by us, step by step. According to the modern principle of division of labor. Professional workers made it all possible, each active in his own sphere. A kind of professional specialization leading to moral blindness. I dare to offer a comparison, one that is not meant to equate anything, but only to express a sense of what is called scientific thinking: scientists discover the possibility of producing weapons by which all of humanity can be wiped out. They do this in all innocence. They are legitimized. Our National So-

---

[1] A reference to West German debates in the late 1970s on whether there should be a statute of limitations for Nazi crimes.

cialists likewise had their professionals with their heads in the sand, who made racism into a scientific discipline. Many worked on the legitimization of this belief in their own highly specialized disciplines. Scientists were involved in the construction of the death camps. One of these, who was involved at Auschwitz, was called Dr. Faust. And people had to be restructured into accomplices in mass murder, and at every level, from simple-minded diligence to subtle cynicism. Our entire society collaborated in Auschwitz. But this is an idea that we do not handle so well. A Frenchman or an American can absorb the pictures of Auschwitz into his consciousness in a different way than we can. He doesn't have to think: we human beings! He can think: those Germans! Can we think: those Nazis? I can't do it. This guilt arose through the conditions of our history. We have inherited this entire history. Not only the patent offices and the state museums. We are the inheritors — also of the conditions that led to Auschwitz. That doesn't mean that we would be capable of doing such a thing again. It only means that it is not enough to wince at the frightful power of these images and then immediately to seek an escape through legalities. Surely there is no conduct that corresponds to what was done in Auschwitz. Even the grotesque attempt to argue away one million or two million dead victims is only further proof that there is no correct way of acting. We are all subject to the temptation of defending ourselves against Auschwitz. We look toward it, and then immediately we look away. It's not possible to live with such images. The victims and the perpetrators still stand on two different sides. There are organizations to promote reconciliation. There are attempts to prevent shame from turning into paralysis. There are endeavors to exculpate the guilt of those alive today. All this is better than nothing. But all this does not allay the struggle within each of us. During our lifetimes there can be no relationship to Auschwitz. For me there is no standpoint I could achieve that would allow me to have a firm opinion about what was done there, or at least a feeling that would be worthy of recognition from the side of the victims and still bearable on the side of the perpetrators. Every image of Auschwitz destroys every possible settlement with this past, a past that remains present. No German can raise himself above this common ground and say that his countrymen who worked here were psychopaths or specialists with whom he has nothing to do. Are we not psychopaths, not specialists? What we have in common with them is our unease, our success, our sense of decorum, our sense of our own righteousness, our enormous trust in our reason. Not that we should demonstrate a kind of conscience that we don't possess, but we should at least admit: Auschwitz cannot be mastered. The fact that after all that

happened we came up with this term anyway: mastering the past! Neither
God nor the humanism that came afterward kept us from committing
the crimes of Auschwitz and then shifting to the notion of mastering this
past.[2] If one observes this sequence of events, one can say from experience that something is lacking in us. Something that both God and humanism intended. Something that transcends the individual. Something
to which the individual is obligated. Something that would have made
this individual incapable of participating in any way in the Auschwitz
murder-factory. Something that God and humanism have not yet
created. We freed ourselves too soon. Every one of us can experience this
when confronted with the images of Auschwitz: we must allow the trial[3]
to continue. Throughout our life. The trial within ourselves. Singing in
chorus we can find no key in which we can speak of Auschwitz. And as
individuals we can only admit to ourselves that we are not equipped to
bear the guilt of Auschwitz. That is: after all the liberal or emancipatory
acts designed to relieve us of our guilt, we find that we are people who
can't be prosecuted. In the face of Auschwitz we learn that as individuals
we are inclined to deny our guilt; everything that might transcend our
individuality, which in the meantime has acquired diamond-like hard-
ness, we reject as obsolete or irrational. . . .

These are confessions that can force their way into an individual's
consciousness in the face of images of Auschwitz. Proud of our non-
binding pluralism, we would have to admit that as individuals we cannot
bear what we have in the way of history. To do this requires transcendent
elements, solidarity — which are foreign words. What was done com-
munally cannot be borne by individuals. Thus the confusion and the
repression. And all the formality with regard to Auschwitz. The survivors
and the families of victims see themselves, as if through an opera staging
trick, confronted with individuals emancipated from any responsibility.
Germans, what are they? East Germans? West Germans? The German
Volk? Never heard of it. At most we're Franconians or Westphalians, citizens of Cologne, Berlin, or Stuttgart. But not Germans: that firm went
bankrupt in 1945. The survivors are Siemens, Deutsche Bank, AEG,
Bayer, BASF, Flick, Hoesch, Thyssen . . . All right, some of these com-
panies were also involved in Auschwitz. But what's a company? Does a

[2] The term "Vergangenheitsbewältigung" (mastering or coming to terms with the past)
is the one generally used to describe the attempts of postwar Germans to deal with
the Nazi past; Walser here breaks the term apart in saying "Bewältigung der Ver-
gangenheit," and returns later to the concept of "bewältigen" or mastering.

[3] The German word "Prozess" means both "trial" and "process," and Walser is clearly
playing on both meanings in this passage.

company have a memory, a conscience? A company is not a moral agent. Someone can be a banker and a business director under Hitler and under Adenauer, and . . . all that people have to change is the uniform that legitimizes them. So there's no hiatus. Only a collapse.[4] Then a rebuilding. A legal successor who pays, organizes, celebrates, and commemorates as well as he can: that is, he has an appointment calendar that masters[5] all. And what about us? We allow ourselves to be mastered. All of us. We are much closer to each other than would be comfortable to the professional haberdashers, those who deliver our indistinguishability, the producers of our individuality. Auschwitz forces us all onto one spot. However we reacted to Auschwitz. . . we still have to admit to ourselves: it shows how closely together we stand. It's bad enough that it is only through what is worst of all, through the guilt of Auschwitz, that our commonality can be pointed out to us. The pictures from Auschwitz show the opposite of what becomes visible in the courtroom: in the courtroom the perpetrators are individuals and the victims legion. In the pictures of Auschwitz the victims are individual human beings and the perpetrators a nation. The individual of today has emancipated himself from the nation. The individual is a member of society and allows the mastering to proceed. The individual pays for this mastering through his semi-official activity. This "mastering" belongs to the same division of labor that made Auschwitz possible — to the system of delegating. But confessing, repenting, praying —we can't do these any more either. Thinking about our own culpability — are we capable of that? Reflecting on our own accountability — could that be called for? This may be achievable not merely through our ability to achieve and to enjoy ourselves, but also through our capacity to belong: through solidarity. I believe that even the memory of the victims, and especially that of the survivors, cannot be served when a crime of this magnitude is assigned ex post facto to a couple of scoundrels. What kind of division is this: I belong to this community as long as we're talking about Goethe's *Faust*, but I have nothing in common with Dr. Faust in Auschwitz. We have everything in common with him that we have in common with Goethe. It seems to me dangerous for all ages and for the future if societies, peoples, states employ all of their power and strength to legitimize and commit crimes and then select perpetrators to bear the responsibility.

[4] The text plays on the relation between "Bruch" (break or hiatus) and "Zusammen-bruch" (collapse).

[5] Here he returns once more to the concept of "bewältigen" or "mastering" — see footnote 1.

In an age in which the great crimes of perpetrators above the individual level are committed under the guise of a kind of legality, it no longer suffices to exempt oneself as an individual and to make conscience the concern of administrators for whom one is responsible only as a taxpayer. The public demonstration of Minister President Filbinger's dearth of experience was a public spectacle that needed no Sophocles to produce a shattering effect.[6] Clearly a powerful machine of education and culture is at work, one that produces good conscience, delivering it even into the hands of a judge who pronounces death sentences.

I believe that one is a criminal if the society to which one belongs commits criminal acts. In Auschwitz we have provided an example of this. No one can tell us how to deal with the knowledge of this culpability. To what extent and with what consequences one regards oneself as belonging to this, and thus as accountable, is for each individual to decide. There can be no prescriptions regarding this. Everything that someone says or does is an acknowledgment. An acknowledgment, in contrast to a confession, takes place not for others and before others, but before oneself and for oneself.

One glance at a picture from Auschwitz suffices for all at least to admit to themselves: we're not done with this. Whatever you do with it, you can't delegate it to others. You cannot allow yourself to be mastered. The power that appears in these pictures emanated from you, and now it returns to you. It is not enough to ask your parents or grandparents how this or that was. Ask yourself: how is it now.

I'd always prefer to look away from these pictures. I have to force myself to look at them. And I know how I have to force myself. If I haven't forced myself for a while to look at them, I notice how I begin to run to seed, to lose my moral compass. And when I do force myself to look, I am aware that I do it for the sake of my accountability.

[6] Hans Filbinger was a prominent West German politician whose past as a judge under the Nazi regime became the subject of much public controversy, prompting him to utter the controversial statement "What was legal back then cannot be illegal now."

Commentary

I N MANY RESPECTS this 1979 speech recapitulates and further develops themes that were broached in the 1965 essay. First and foremost, Walser delves into the issue of the collective responsibility Germans bear for the Holocaust, and he delivers an even harsher verdict than before, asserting early on: "Our entire society collaborated in Auschwitz," and toward the end of the speech stating: "I believe that one is a criminal if the society to which one belongs commits criminal acts." He speaks again of the widespread belief among the German public that by punishing those most directly involved in perpetrating atrocities — for instance, the Auschwitz functionaries — this collective guilt can be alleviated, and once again he calls this belief an illusion. He even seems to suggest that punishing such individuals is justified only by the understandable desire of the survivors and families of victims for justice, but that it is in some ways questionable. The question of how these individuals came to be capable of such actions becomes absorbed into the larger question of how German society shaped them to this end. In insisting on the idea of collective guilt, he seems even to question the notion of individual guilt: "It is impossible for the individual to bear pure guilt." He suggests that modern society's structural principles of division of labor and professional specialization helped make the horrors possible ("A kind of professional specialization leading to moral blindness"). He then refers to Nazi ideologues who "made racism into a scientific discipline," and compares them to scientists whose research led to the discovery of weapons of mass destruction. Though he hastens to add that he is not equating the two situations, he is nevertheless comparing those who theorized racism with scientists conducting research, the point being that what might be labeled in either case as an intellectual enterprise leads, at least potentially, to horrendously murderous consequences. Despite his disclaimer, this comparison seems rather unsettling.

But whereas in the 1965 essay he used the first-person pronoun "we" to acknowledge his belonging to the community of perpetrators, but still clearly assumed a morally superior stance in castigating his fellow Germans for their moral blindness, here his use of the pronoun seems more genuine, in that the speech is devoted largely to exploring the agony experienced by Germans, himself included, in contemplating their responsibility for Auschwitz, as he had admonished them to do earlier. Both the title of the speech and his comments at the start emphasize the notion of Auschwitz as a constant presence in the life and consciousness of every German, something that can never be "mastered." The phrase in the title ". . . und kein Ende" generally suggests a kind of impatience with something that has gone on too long, and this sense is conveyed in much of the speech as well. In one very telling passage, he says:

> A Frenchman or an American can absorb the pictures of Auschwitz into his consciousness in a different way than we can. He doesn't have to think: we human beings! He can think: those Germans! Can we think: those Nazis? I can't do it. This guilt arose through the conditions of our history. We have inherited this entire history.

Given the complicity of many non-Germans in perpetrating the Holocaust, one might well reply that if French, Americans, and other nationalities respond to images of the Holocaust only by pointing the finger at Germans, they instead might well reflect on the complicity of their own nations,[7] and on their own individual potential for evil. But Walser does not take this step: his insistence that responsibility for the Holocaust rests solely on German shoulders may seem admirable in one sense, but it might be observed that Germans are thus assigned a rather crushing burden that no other nation must shoulder.

The question of German national identity looms large in the speech. Delving into the question of what Germans at the present time have in common with Holocaust perpetrators, he says:

> No German can raise himself above this common ground and say that his countrymen who worked here were psychopaths or specialists with whom he has nothing to do. Are we not psychopaths, not specialists? What we have in common with them is our unease, our success, our sense of decorum, our sense of our own righteousness, our enormous trust in our reason.

He thus radically rejects any attempt to assert a distance between the perpetrators and "ordinary Germans." But then he points out that Germans try to evade their responsibility by retreating into local or regional identities: "Germans, what are they? East Germans? West Germans? The German *Volk*? Never heard of it. At most we're Franconians or Westphalians, citizens of Cologne, Berlin, or Stuttgart. But not Germans: that firm went bankrupt in 1945." It is interesting to note that this regionalism is placed side by side with the East-West division of Germany, an issue that will assume central importance in the following

---

[7] For instance, the cooperation of French officials under the Pétain regime in rounding up and deporting French Jews, and the American refusal to admit hundreds of Jewish refugees aboard the S.S. St. Louis in 1939.

two texts. But what is most striking about his assertion of a shared German identity is his assertion of what constitutes that identity, namely the shared guilt for the Holocaust: "Auschwitz forces us all onto one spot . . . it is only through what is worst of all, through the guilt of Auschwitz, that our commonality can be pointed out to us."

He heaps scorn on the concept of "Vergangenheitsbewältigung" or mastering the past, stating flatly: "Auschwitz cannot be mastered." He even suggests at one point: "This 'mastering' belongs to the same division of labor that made Auschwitz possible — to the system of delegating."

A related issue is that of the relationship between the individual and the collective, raised initially with regard to the Holocaust perpetrators but then extended to deal with the plight of contemporary Germans. As quoted earlier, he questions whether it is possible for an individual to bear "pure guilt" and then suggests that for a collectivity to do so is even more difficult. He speaks critically of the increasing cult of individualism he sees: "The individual of today has emancipated himself from the nation." He says further that "it no longer suffices to exempt oneself as an individual and to make conscience the concern of administrators for whom one is responsible only as a taxpayer." This would suggest that the retreat to individual isolation is an escape from the necessary task of facing collective responsibility. Yet at the same time he questions whether this collective responsibility or guilt can ever be mastered, and ends the speech with a return to his individual sense of struggle. This ambiguity will reemerge in the following texts.

At the end of the speech he speaks of his own desire to look away from the images of Auschwitz, and his sense that he must force himself to look, "for the sake of my accountability." As pointed out earlier, this suggests most pointedly the change in his stance from the 1965 essay: whereas in the earlier essay he used the pronoun "we" rhetorically but clearly assumed the position of someone criticizing or preaching to the collective indicated by that pronoun, here he admits that he shares in all the moral and psychological conundrums of his fellow Germans.

But once again a troubling theme emerges, namely that of the gulf separating victims and perpetrators. Early in the speech he says:

> The victims and the perpetrators still stand on two different sides. There are organizations to promote reconciliation. There are attempts to prevent shame from turning into paralysis. There are endeavors to exculpate the guilt of those alive today. All this is better than nothing. But all this does not allay the struggle within each of us.

Lumping together "organizations to promote reconciliation" with attempts to alleviate the shame and guilt of Germans, he offers lukewarm support to such efforts — more positive, at any rate, than his dismissive reference to "the pathetic attempt to place ourselves on the side of the victim" in the 1965 essay — but suggests that there is little to be hoped from such endeavors. The Germans are thus condemned to bear a burden of guilt, one that cannot be mastered, and that remains fresh thirty-five years later.

Handshake with Ghosts (1979)

Context

IN THE SAME YEAR as the preceding speech (1979), Walser published an essay that, unlike the previous two texts, makes no overt reference to Auschwitz in its title; in fact, the title "Handshake with Ghosts" is deliberately mystifying, and suggestive of the more ambiguous and "literary" nature of the text that follows. Ironically, since one of the themes of the essay is the problematic role of the "public intellectual" in West Germany, the essay appeared in a collection edited by Jürgen Habermas, who is himself the epitome of the public intellectual and who thematizes the concept of the public sphere in much of his writing.

Walser's withdrawal from political engagement, which started around the mid-1970s, was also reflected in a shift from drama to prose as his primary sphere of literary production. In a 1986 interview he said:

> For me the novel is a kind of intimate unfolding of consciousness, and it can achieve political relevance only in a highly indirect manner. But it's a different story with drama, with theater plays. Public speech on stage can be overtly political.[1]

His association of his preferred literary mode of the last thirty years — prose fiction — with a very personal and only indirectly political stance is highly revealing, because the texts that make up the remainder of this volume — "Handshake with Ghosts" (1979), "Speaking of Germany" (1988), the Peace Prize Speech (1998), and "On Talking to Yourself" (2000) — all show clear signs of this "literary" stance, combined with a reluctance to adopt the role of public speaker, as he had in the 1965 essay.

---

[1] From an interview with Günter Gaus, cited in Gerald A. Fetz, *Martin Walser* (Stuttgart and Weimar: J. B. Metzler, 1997), 10.

If German identity emerged as a significant secondary theme in the speech "No End to Auschwitz," it assumes central importance in this essay. Walser, who had been widely identified as a classic left-wing intellectual and even castigated in the conservative press for his association with the Communist Party around 1970, here enters into a discourse on German national identity that would increasingly isolate him from his former colleagues on the left. The "politically correct" view of the division of Germany among those on the left in West Germany might be summarized as follows: it is very sad, but we deserve it as a punishment for the crimes of the Nazi regime, and we must accept it and move on. In the sixties, Walser too had adopted this position; in fact, Jörg Magenau points out that he refused to protest against the building of the Berlin Wall in 1961.[2] In the 1950s and 1960s it was primarily conservative Christian Democratic politicians who spoke of reunification, though it might be questioned whether any really believed it to be an attainable goal.

The previous year, in a speech given in Bergen-Enkheim (near Frankfurt am Main), Walser had already created a stir by stating: "We ought . . . to grant as little recognition to West Germany as we do to East Germany. We must keep open the wound called Germany." In the essay that follows he takes up this theme and connects it to the issue of the tension between private and public opinion.

[2] Magenau, *Martin Walser: Eine Biographie* (Reinbek bei Hamburg: Rowohlt, 2005), 178.

Martin Walser: Handshake with Ghosts (1979)

I MARVEL AT THE MORAL EXHAUSTION[3] I see today. Even if some people say I was a hypocrite in the days when I felt more vigorous, still I don't think it's a pleasant development that I have less and less desire or strength for hypocrisy in recent times. Hypocrisy — that is, the time when I made greater demands on myself and on others — was, or so I believe, more humane than the compliant depravity I now experience. It is a growing wild, but without the natural charm that a garden acquires when one ceases to tend it. Sometimes it seems as if we're heading toward a complete lack of cultivation, toward pure evil. It's enough to shake one up in anticipation.

Do many people feel the same way? Does the sum of all those who feel the same amount to a major shift in trends of thinking? How can I explain my newest inclination to myself? Can I still offer resistance, or must I plow ahead? Do I have to let myself become immune to possible feelings of disgust toward others? Must I too fall into these auto-erotic baby motions and drain them linguistically? And join in the chorus of Titanic bel canto? And keep silent about the comical nature of this well-situated cultivation of misfortune? Yes. One is part of it. One should not appear to oneself as something special. But to be part of it today means precisely to feel special. Do I feel special? To answer this first-person-singular question by saying "no" seems superfluous.

It's a question of the personal component that statements made in the first person have or don't have (or that they are supposed to have or not to have).

If, as a co-worker in the creation of public opinion, one has for years tried to achieve a social mode of expression (as opposed to a narcissistic one), the danger arises that the mode of expression takes on a life of its own and has less and less to do with the person practicing it.

It's advisable to remain in the third person for the time being. Just because continuing in the first person easily loses credibility. So: a person cannot take back the opinions that he expressed publicly, but neither can he present them as he did ten years earlier. He and his opinions have become somewhat estranged from one another. He doesn't think differently than he did ten years ago, but he's become less sensitive in the face of the difficulties into which his political aspirations have led. His

---

[3] Walser uses the term "Ermüdbarkeit," literally "exhaustibility" or a proclivity to become exhausted.

opinion must, so to speak, do without him. He does almost nothing any more as a public spokesman to help promote the development of our society toward democracy. Sometimes he even leaves the cries for help from victims of dictatorships still in power lying on his desk until the paper has turned yellow with age; then he discards them. Again and again he feels clearly enough that he ought to participate in political actions in support of Horst Mahler, who is now sitting in prison as the victim of an unjust legal judgment.[4] Everyone knows about this. But you just can't shake yourself into motion. The fact that a protest that is only in written form may be ineffective did not prevent you from signing it ten years ago. So now he clearly has joined the band of intellectuals who are trying to lend a purely personal expression to their public face. Obviously egotism, that lifelong childhood illness of intellectuals, has increased in him. This disturbs his self-image. The reactions of others have presented him to himself as a "left-wing intellectual." Someone like that ought to be, if not immune, then at least not completely defenseless against egotism. After all, he wants to be a democrat with a claim to realizing his goals, and thus a socialist. He didn't start out with labels like this, but rather with experiences conditioned by his generation and his origins. His generation and his origins dispose him to be a democrat with a claim to realizing his goals, and thus a socialist. That's what he still has to call his banner. (What a relief that he doesn't have to say that in the first person!) And nevertheless he doesn't really stand up for anything any more; he even notices that within him a distance has arisen from himself. Without wanting or being able to take back or even correct the opinions that he has published often enough — so he doesn't have the compulsion to make fun now of what he thought ten years ago, and of those who almost took him seriously back then, in that respect he doesn't measure up to a certain important colleague — still he has to admit that his published opinions do not entirely express what is inside him. So they're not right. A large part of his consciousness never entered into these published opinions. A self-inflicted samizdat[5] has arisen inside

[4] At the time of this essay Horst Mahler was a prominent attorney who defended and supported left-wing militants and then became involved in the RAF (Red Army Faction) and was imprisoned for his role in planning their bank heists. Ironically, in the 1980s he did a political about-face and became a prominent figure in ultra-nationalist and antisemitic circles.

[5] A Russian word designating the secret publication of materials considered subversive by the Soviet regime. Walser's usage of the term emphasizes the situation of having thoughts and feelings that cannot be publicly expressed, rather than the fact of their publication.

him. This has become so clear in the meantime that he's had the feeling for some time now that he's withholding something. But can one really always say EVERYTHING? When the issue is a particular, usually current aspect of our development toward democracy, who is interested in the personal component, even if it is still so powerful? I'm posing this question now, because our public opinion, if everyone felt the same way as he does, or rather I do, might be quite a work of art, or a rather artificial construct.[6] After *God* we haven't had anything more important than the *public sphere*. That's why it must be of importance to us that public opinion, which is regarded by political scientists as our political culture's source of legitimization, be full of reality and not increasingly a product of lip service by paid specialists. To what extent are we still inside our public opinion? If one of us constantly writes commentaries on foreign policy or theater reviews or articles about nuclear power plants or essays on purely theological matters, or about sports, or about music, or about economic policy . . . what does he then still have to do with what he has written? How does it still concern him? Doesn't what has been withheld grow ever larger with each publication? And in that case what kind of democratic development would this be? Or is this difference between what is withheld and what is published unproblematic? Or do our true sentiments permeate our opinions by their own force, so that we needn't concern ourselves about this? Marx, it's said, based his thinking on a similar assumption. Public opinion in the Soviet satellite states proves through its ludicrously artificial uniformity, even more blatantly than does our artificial diversity of opinion, that the development toward democracy exacts a high price in nerves and decades, without making even the slightest progress in the direction of one's goal. In that case, public opinion wasn't really any opinion at all. No process that deserves to be called democratic seems to have been in motion. That appears to be the case when we judge by what the media allow to appear. Samizdat always seems necessary for the true expression of current reality. With us, everyone (if my case is typical) has his own samizdat. Before I try to get closer to my own by way of confessions, mention must be made of the harm that can arise when our public opinion is a routine object created and controlled by mandarins. Pluralism as a patchwork body laid out for public view, that's our ideal. As many colors as possible, as inconsequential as possible, as public as possible: that's the credo of the press.

---

[6] There is a wordplay in the German that is lost in translation: the word "ziemlich" can mean either "considerable" or "proper" (as in the first phrase) or (adverbially, as in the second phrase) "rather" or "somewhat."

Democratic development would only flourish, I believe, if real con-tradictions could really become public. But between two leading op-ed columnists who confront each other with opposing standpoints, a real contradiction never arises, since their columns are essentially similar: they are op-ed columns first and foremost, just as white and black horses are first and foremost horses. There's no real contradiction there. There would be one, I hope, if a column contained a contradiction within itself — if it were in conflict with itself. Then it could also stand in conflict with another. But a column that was in conflict with itself would no longer be an op-ed column. A theater review that really expressed the reviewer's sentiments would no longer be viewed as a theater review. And a public opinion that consists of purely monochromatic elements simulates diversity, just as the opinion published in the eastern zones simulates a public sphere. The public sphere in the East appears to me as a shabby theater production. Our pluralism has reality to the same extent that a jungle produced in a Disney studio contains nature. In movie studios there are experts for tiger paws, velvet paws, clouds, and violets — but it's all just animated.

People far more knowledgeable than I determined long ago how public opinion is endangered by the fact that it derives from group and class interests. I'm just talking about the danger that threatens the nec-essary realism of public opinion because each one of us, due to a special reservation, conceals his own individuality, or something that is indi-vidual. It never seems to be appropriate to mention it in the discussion.

My development toward small-mindedness, for example. I've con-cealed that development up to now, because I fear it might be called narrow-mindedness.

That's why I prefer the milder third-person form: it's a question of something that awaits him. Something that has already consumed him. But he doesn't entirely agree with it yet. Sometimes he still resists it. Then he tries to legitimize what is happening to him. He doesn't know if it's the fault of the weather, the meal, or the first page of his daily paper. Sometimes he's ashamed of his development and tries to suppress it en-tirely; at other times he defends it vehemently against the concerned or acerbic arguments of friends. For example, thus: Well, isn't one's cons-ciousness allowed to exist in the form it's taken on after all this time, more involuntarily than voluntarily? Is he doing anything other than allowing his consciousness to swing into its own position? Finally no more criticism of one's own inclination, but instead acceptance of an inclination that one previously had fought constantly. Allowing the contradiction to exist, finally! A sudden letting-in of thought-ghosts and opinion-monsters that for years have been fought off and have been insisting on being let in. But that would mean keeping silent. Soon he would no longer be allowed to tell anyone what he "really" thinks. Did he ever do that? After all, he had always seen the devils outside his windows and doors and keyholes and door chinks, and he had always fought them off. But he never told anyone else that they were laying siege to him and threatening him. He acted as though he were already out of the woods! As if he himself did not contain all the evils he is fighting! He wanted to be a sentry of progress, of an approach to humanity. He lived in a tense condition. Between atavisms that were pulling him downward, and the contemporary necessity of freeing himself from the bad baggage of his heritage and tradition. Now, weary and capitulating, could he be taken captive in the twinkling of an eye by that barbarism of the past? Might the handshake with ghosts have taken place? Now he tells himself — and, in order to seduce himself, he calls it a confession — that he was never free of the burdens of the past; he only *wanted* to move on, but he never succeeded in moving on; but that isn't his fault.

What are the ghosts that want to be let in? The worst ones will reveal themselves only once they are inside. A few are impertinent enough to reveal themselves while they are still knocking on the doors and windows. He refuses to name them! Thus speaks the former master of lip service. The truth is that he doesn't dare to admit to their names. He also fears that by speaking their names out loud he would in a sense establish them in his consciousness. That too is only evasion, cowardice. The ghosts have been made taboo. With his help. He's afraid. One time, as an experiment, he pretends to be ashamed of what may be waiting for him. But is it shame at all? Or is it a sort of coquetry? Now he says that not everything he excluded formerly may be excluded completely. He excluded contradictions. After all, opinions are feelings too. They really aren't unambiguous. So now it must be confessed: in every, truly in *every* case in which an opinion is expressed unambiguously, what is done is to create illusion instead of helping reality to find expression. Illusion wants everything to occur more quickly. The process should be direct. The result: processes that exist only in appearance, ceremonies of democracy *en masse*. Then reality unfolds its own real existence. The mandarin is frightened. The glass in the temple trembles.

In notebooks, insofar as they aren't intended for publication, things might always look a bit more realistic. I quote what I wrote on March 25, 1975 in my notebook, in which I record my daily exercises:

I have a disturbed relationship to reality. I have to admit that. Thus
whatever I say can easily be dismissed. I'd like to prove, or at least maintain, that my disturbed relationship to reality has something to do with
the fact that I am a German and I was born in the year 1927. I don't
believe that a German of my generation can have an undisturbed relationship to reality. Our national reality is itself disturbed. And when
something so decisive is disturbed, it's possible that one cannot trust
anything derived from it. What I lack above all is trust. But it seems to
me that this is due not to me but to circumstances. Those of the nation.
They don't allow for trust. This nation, in its divided state, is a constant
source of trust-destruction. This nation contradicts itself. I am incapable
of thinking and experiencing only as a citizen of West Germany just
because I reside in West Germany. But even less can I adopt East Germany as my own. I cannot defend either German state, either within myself or in general. Every process of identification that might be called
natural — one that might proceed by itself every day and lead to greater
and greater feelings of belonging — is constantly destroyed by the other
part of the nation. Gradually I learn that only one form of identification
remains: an identification with the contradiction between the two German states. The only thing that is justified seems to me the sharpness
with which they contradict each other. But I cannot identify at all with
this contradiction in its content. What East Germany condemns West
Germany for seems exaggerated to me; it says much more about the East
than it does about the West. And the opposite is equally true. The image
that is painted here in the West, of East Germany as a prison, is supposed
to convince our people to feel free in spite of their powerlessness and
coercion. And still I identify with the contradictory relationship that exists between the two states. It seems to me that there is every reason in
the world for the two states to contradict each other, that nothing is as
important as the negation that each one voices to the other, but also that
nothing is so unjustified as the positions from which each state presents
its negation of the other. Am I merely seeking to salve my conscience?
Am I seeking national images to justify my personal situation? Would it
be better to derive the contradictions in which I live from my social class?
Petty bourgeois! Does my disturbed relationship to reality come from the
irreconcilability of the needs for salvation and desires for remuneration on
the part of the petty bourgeois and the reality of the class system that denies fulfillment? I am full of longing for a sense of connectedness. For the
joy of trust. Sometimes I allow myself simply to be attracted by something. Until I am then repelled once more.

Perhaps one can say: the worst is not spoken. Everything that someone says is an attempt to escape the necessity of saying the worst. That's
why everything I say is so harmless. To me, saying something means

concealing something. Should we regard our public opinion as well in light of this caveat?

Still: no language philosophy, please. The commandment suffices: thou shalt not lie. In the attempt to obey this commandment, all possible linguistic problems must arise and be solved.

After all, we ourselves have created the ills that must be borne in this situation. We wanted *only* the best. That's it. It's always been that way. The results are painful. We haven't succeeded in making openness into a rewarding democratic virtue. Highly valued are reticence (and thus the appearance of strength), certainty, and knowledge (and thus hypocrisy). We have given weakness and suffering and helplessness such negative connotations that we cannot inform each other about our real condition any more. Worse than the jargon of authenticity, which is so disdained, is the jargon in which it is disdained.

Language says something only when it is used by the innocent. This state of innocence is not lost once and for all for every intellectual. Necessity always produces it once more. And language, which itself is something created, gives rise to this loss because of our susceptibility to education.[7]

The correct conduct probably can be discussed only in the context of the historical capacity of language. All questionings of language that tend to the systematic seem fathomless to me. Even when they begin ever so modestly with an examination of stuttering and never want to go beyond that in anyone's lifetime. The historically oriented individual is more likely to refuse to use a scientific defense as a substitute for practice.

I sense that our national and social perplexity is a consequence of our alienation from our history.

It seems to me that after 1918 our intellectuals separated themselves from the *Volk,* and that since then they have repressed what was experienced within, with, or through the *Volk.* The word alone evokes multi-faceted shuddering. *Volk* — is that even a concept? Isn't that word totally *obsolete*? Doesn't the notion of a class-based society make everything that has historically been associated with the notion of *Volk* superfluous? And to what class do those ladies and gentlemen belong who worked toward making *Volk* an expression for the gathering together of something common to all? And if we force the necessary expression of this large

---

[7] Walser is here playing with the related words *bilden* (the verb meaning to create or form) and *Bildung* (meaning education or culture).

gathering into such an unreal and ahistorical concept as "collective," does that really represent progress?

The German *Volk* lost the First World War. But the German *Volk* was no more responsible for this war than the English, Russians, French, Italians, or Austrians. The bourgeois-feudal cliques in the countries involved might rather be named as those primarily responsible for this decisive catastrophe. But the consequences had to be borne almost exclusively by the German *Volk*. Not the society. Not a collective. The *Volk*, the German *Volk*, was humiliated and exploited. By the bourgeois-feudal cliques of the victorious powers. The German bourgeois-feudal clique cast its lot, to the extent possible, on the side of the victors, both economically and politically. But one part of this clique didn't succeed in doing this; it proceeded to exploit its resentment and the suffering of the *Volk* for a further adventure that was even worse. Philosophy and literature in the 1920s were, to the extent we take them seriously today, internationally oriented, so right away they were off the hook. The intellectuals had their Roaring Twenties. The workers and petty bourgeois faced a hopeless struggle against the incursions of a capitalism that now appeared truly international. After 1945 we were treated much more leniently, even though we had behaved much worse. That's why after 1945 no rabid "Heil Hitler" movement was nurtured among this *Volk*. But when people looked back at the year 1933, there was almost general agreement that the German *Volk* inclined to the reactionary, the petty-bourgeois, the dull, the anti-Enlightenment, and the proto-Fascist. The intellectuals responsible were either not involved in what happened in 1933 or they were victims. It was once again this German *Volk* that had watched the crimes being committed, had been complicit in them, or had cheered them on. Again, the intellectuals responsible weren't there. They had nothing to do with these fanatical petty bourgeois. And the capitalists are always on the side of the winners of war and history anyway. The dumb fool is always the *Volk*. It learns one lesson after another and still hardly progresses in its learning and relearning. And the German *Volk* is a model student. In East *and* West. It prefers to lose its own self rather than cause the slightest distress to its teacher, East or West. Who are we? "What kind of person is he?" the new servant of Phileas Fogg asks his predecessor in Jules Verne's *Around the World in Eighty Days*. He learns that his future master is above all an Englishman. But who are *we*? As soon as we're abroad, we're Germans. But who am I here at home? And even in Moscow or New York I'm not allowed to be as ruthlessly German as they are Russian or American at home. It's expected of me that I bear my Germanness with a kind of composure, just as you bear a kind of affliction that you can't do anything about, but that you also can't get rid of. When the thoroughly lovable sense of pride with which my conversation partners show their Americanness, or the impressive vehemence with which my conversation partners show their Russianness, induces me to give even a slightly positive spin to my Germanness, I immediately provoke resistance. If not on the part of the other, then within myself.

Auschwitz. There it is. Finished. If we could come to terms with Auschwitz, we could devote ourselves once more to national tasks. But I must admit: a society that is purely secular, a liberal society that shuns the religious and everything that transcends the individual self, can only repress Auschwitz. Where the ego is supreme, one can only repress guilt. One can absorb, retain, and bear it only together with others. But every movement towards togetherness arouses the suspicion of something obsolete. Where ideas like togetherness, solidarity, and nation appear, a child of the liberal world of the Federal Republic sees the church or Communism or Fascism. The up-to-date intellectual rejects history — Beckett is his man. His favorite games are lovely eruptions of egotism, autoerotic babyishness, and the constant celebration of human existence's proneness to suicide. I suspect that since the time of Beckett the loss of history in literature has increased drastically. Or does it just seem that way to me because my starting point is German literature? Is Beckett a favorite writer among Germans on account of his heroic denial of history? Adorno gave a blanket endorsement to this denial of history in his polemical comments against Brecht. The whole apparatus of the culture industry,[8] in its evaluating and dispensing of blessings, has elevated the special case of Beckett, which in itself is quite innocent and unassuming, to the status of path-breaking avant-garde. It seems to me that it's always just Beckett himself who is innocent and justified. His various prophets, though, seem to me people who prefer to find nothing rather than to seek something. When this anti-faction doesn't see a purpose of life blossoming from the waysides and the trees along the path, they say that there is no such purpose. But it could be that purpose is a product, like light, warmth, wheat, and milk. Something that requires appropriate work. And long traditions. And we could say to our customers that the purpose we have is one that's been created. Not a bit more natural than light, warmth, wheat, and milk are in today's world.

---

[8] A term coined by Adorno signifying the manipulation of the masses to adopt cultural values that serve the interests of capitalists.

I believe that it is also our historical deficit that makes us incapable of criticizing the processes to which we see ourselves subjected. For the longest time we've seen ourselves as intimidated and cowardly. Anyone who still manifests social impulses gets his comeuppance. But as soon as someone lets off steam in an egotistical manner, he gets a pat on the head. So all those who need a pat on the head let off steam in the desired manner. For those who hand out the head pats, we can't go far enough with our letting-off of steam. Preferably as far as the incomprehensibility that even Adorno cuddled up with. What hasn't been said in the pages of our most sophisticated newspapers on the subject of our inability to love! And how lovingly is our glittering egotism accompanied by photographs and commentary! And how harshly rebuked is even the slightest comment in a text or in the theater that arose because someone expected himself or his language to fulfill a task. "That's too low-brow!" people say right away. Thus an epoch deludes itself. Farewell to practical action. Farewell to the *Volk*. And I make bold to add: farewell to God. Because God to me is not an obsolete term but rather a historical word for our need to transcend the ego. Nor do I consider this directional goal to be obsolete.

Anyone can see that we're missing something. Maybe that something is what we've suppressed. Internationalism is an equally forced value in East and West Germany. The fact that in each case internationalism gives heed to only one side of the world is never mentioned, because of the otherwise threatening embarrassing word comedy.

Why do we accept a division as if it were a law of nature, even though we can see that it arose from entirely temporal conditions? I admit, if a *Volk* is politically divided through an action that is understandable due to the circumstances, and if this action is successful forever (so to speak), then what was divided was never really a *Volk*. France could never be divided. If we remained West Germany and East Germany, the result would be not German but international. I believe that the specific historic deficit thereby decreed would sooner or later have to make the two societies resulting from this division incapable of consolidating a natural sense of identity that would last from generation to generation. I believe that we and East Germany would by necessity have to reach a common limitation: both sides would be lacking in depth. Since I have been making use of a number of *obsolete* terms, no one should be surprised that I use this term, which points both back into history and down into the soil.

Of course it's possible that the lack I'm trying to express exists only within myself. Perhaps everyone else is fulfilled, optimistic about the future, and in a good mood. West Germans forever. In that case the political situation can remain in its current state. Collective bargaining, market economy, either freedom of opinion or restrictions on artistic expression: the different spheres can live with this. Then you can forget I said anything. Then I'm self-deluded. Then my ghosts really are ghosts. My anxiety, nothing but a passing mood. And it'll be gone right away. From a hardly moving shadow it changes into a still night. Then a certain music enters once more. I'm back. In West Germany. In this republic of ours there's a furious effort made to justify a temporary state of affairs. Contradiction to this is desired only as something ahistorical, as a radically unhappy gesture, as a hopeless and therefore modest sort of egotistical eccentricity. I have a need to overcome historically the condition known as West Germany. We should start afresh and proceed forward. But the reigning public opinion, the dominant way of thinking, the predominant form of speech all call this need *obsolete*, meaning outdated; I think it's just old.

Commentary

WHERE THE FIRST TWO TEXTS we have examined — "Our Auschwitz" and "No End to Auschwitz" — for the most part avoid the first person, speaking instead about moral or social issues in broad terms or of Germans as a collective, this essay begins with a first-person pronoun, and this is suggestive of the general manner and theme of the text that follows. One could see this as a continuation of the speech of the same year, which in its final paragraph does retreat to the first person, as Walser confesses his own desire to look away from Auschwitz images, while stating that he regards it as a moral imperative to resist this temptation. More strikingly, he uses the same verb "verwildern" (to grow wild) as a metaphor in the final paragraph of the speech and in the opening paragraph of this essay. In the Auschwitz speech, this "verwildern" is associated with the avoidance of dealing with the legacy of German guilt. In this essay, it is associated with the fact "that I have less and less desire or strength for hypocrisy in recent times." He then proceeds to define hypocrisy as "the time when I made greater demands on myself and on others." The reader is thus confronted from the start with an apparent contradiction: hypocrisy is generally understood to be a negative term, but in defining it as he does, he makes it appear more desirable than its opposite, namely to make no demands on oneself or on others, which he calls "compliant depravity." This paradox signals a central theme of the text. On the one hand he claims that he does not renounce the political or moral positions he has assumed in the past; at the same time, though, he is suggesting that there is something inauthentic about them.

In the next paragraph he indicates (through a series of rhetorical questions) that his own withdrawal into the private sphere is symptomatic of a more general trend, which he speaks of in disparaging terms such as "auto-erotic baby motions" and "Titanic bel canto," the latter term suggesting also a blindness to impending catastrophe. He says that in light of the fact that one (here he switches to an impersonal form) is part of this larger trend one shouldn't act as if one were special, but then he mockingly points out that considering oneself special is a feature of the culture of the day: "to be part of it today means precisely to feel special." He speaks of his own past as a "as a co-worker in the creation of public opinion," during which he has "tried to achieve a social mode of expression (as opposed to a narcissistic one)," then points out the danger that this form of expression may separate itself from the speaker and thus become inauthentic. He concludes from this that it is advisable to remain in the third person, which he does for most of the remainder of the essay. But it is clear that, unlike the third-person forms in the previous texts, the third person here is used as a literary device, a deliberate means of distancing the speaker or writer from the text.

In the following paragraph, he speaks in some detail about his personal evolution (though in the third person throughout) from a committed public intellectual to a withdrawn writer who is reluctant to intervene in political issues. He seems to reproach himself for his failure to respond to appeals from victims of foreign dictatorships or of victims of injustice in Germany: "Obviously egotism, that lifelong childhood illness of intellectuals, has increased in him." He reflects that this threatens his self-image, which is based on ideological labels: "a democrat with a claim to realizing his goals, and thus a socialist." Though he does not renounce these labels, his ambivalence is clear from the fact that he speaks first of his own self-image and then suggests that these labels were assigned to him through the perceptions of others. The problem is that his starting point is not the ideological positions indicated by these labels but the experiences he has had due to his generation and his nationality (in the diary fragment from which he quotes later on, he explicitly refers to himself as a German born in 1927). Thus his public statements, which arise from the "banner" he has chosen and/or been assigned, do not fully express who he is. But he draws the conclusion from this that they are not only incomplete but also not right. He makes the first of several references to a "samizdat," thus equating himself with a writer in the Soviet Union who fears the consequences of publicizing his views and thus must publish in private presses.

To justify what might seem to be a rather extreme claim to make about his position as a writer in a reasonably democratic society, he makes the statement: "After *God* we haven't had anything more important than the *public sphere*." This is first an indirect critique of the dogmatic secularism of German society, but it is also a claim that public discourse has assumed the place once accorded to religion in society. It is for this reason, he argues, that it is crucial that this public discourse be authentic: in other words, that the true feelings of those who participate in this discourse not be withheld in order to conform with the ideological stance one has assumed, or with public expectations. And yet the trend is precisely the reverse: "Does not what has been withheld grow ever larger with each publication?" He mocks both the enforced uniformity of public discourse in East Germany and the apparent diversity of public opinion in the West, which he dismisses as a kind of patchwork pluralism. Two opposing op-ed columns, he suggests, do not constitute diversity, since they are essentially alike in being one-sided op-ed columns. True diversity, and true democratic discourse, would arise only "if real contradictions could really become public," in other words if each individual utterance were allowed and encouraged to express all the conflicting sentiments within that individual.

He begins the next section by referring to the "more knowledge-able" individuals who have pointed out the danger that arises from the fact that public opinion is determined by class interests. The Marxist terminology he employs here evokes a passage earlier in the essay in which he cites Marx specifically. What is notable both times is that he does not specifically refute this position — one that he might be assumed to share, considering his well-known identification with the West German left — but suggests instead that it is beside the point, that it doesn't address the real issue, which is the inauthenticity of public opinion due to the withholding of the personal element. Here he returns briefly to the first person, referring ironically to "my development toward small-mindedness," but then reasserts the advisability of remaining in the third person. He speaks of the arguments he has had with friends due to his recent evolution, and asks: "Isn't one's consciousness allowed to exist in the form it it's taken on after all this time, more involuntarily than voluntarily?" This seems a rhetorical question, since it would appear obvious that one is entitled to the feelings and opinions that one has developed through one's life's experiences. But then, once again creating an aura of ambiguity, he refers to this development as "a sudden letting-in of thought-ghosts and opinion-monsters that for years have been fought off and have been insisting on being let in." From the stance of an independent-minded thinker who refuses to conform to social pressures, he switches to that of an individual who tries to ward off (as yet unnamed) ghosts and monsters.

What are these ghosts? The answer emerges in the following passage:

> He wanted to be a sentry of progress, of an approach to humanity. He lived in a tense condition. Between atavisms that were pulling him downward, and the contemporary necessity of freeing himself from the bad baggage of his heritage and tradition. Now, weary and capitulating, could he be taken captive in the twinkling of an eye by that barbarism of the past? Might the handshake with ghosts have taken place?

Clearly the "ghosts" in question are those of the German past, which is here characterized as "the bad baggage of his heritage and tradition" and "barbarism." But if at first he suggests that these ghosts are indeed to be resisted at all costs, he then confesses that it is because of his lack of courage that he does not name them, for the reason that "The ghosts have been made taboo. With his help." This is a key passage, for it suggests not only that what he had just disdained as "the bad baggage of his heritage and tradition" is in fact the national heritage of all Germans, but also that this heritage has been made taboo by the discourse of public intellectuals to which he himself has contributed.

At this point, he launches into an extended discussion of the division of Germany and his own unwillingness to accept that division, thus recapitulating the stance he took in a speech of the previous year, a stance that in the following years would create an ever greater gap between him and his former colleagues on the left. He uses several devices to distance himself from his statements, first quoting at length from his diary, in which he speaks of his "disturbed relationship to reality," but then adds: "I don't believe that a German of my generation can have an undisturbed relationship to reality." This is due in large part to Germany's division: "This nation, in its divided state, is a constant source of trust-destruction." He states that he cannot identify as a resident of the West Germany, any more than he can identify with East Germany. The only form of identification remaining, he asserts, is one "with the contradiction between the two German states."

In the pages that follow he examines the difficulties in asserting a collective German identity, and while surveying German history since 1918 he focuses on two problems: generally, the "alienation from our history," thus the difficulty experienced by all Germans in accepting their past, and more particularly, the alienation of German intellectuals since 1918 from the German *Volk* — a term he uses in conscious defiance of the distaste it evokes from precisely these intellectuals. Interestingly, he tries to adopt his earlier Marxist paradigm to support this position: "The capitalists are always on the side of the winners of war and history anyway. The dumb fool is always the *Volk*." Why is it, he asks, that Germans when abroad feel constrained to contain or hide the characteristics of their national identity in a way that Russians and Americans are not? The answer:

> Auschwitz. There it is. Finished. If we could come to terms with Auschwitz, we could devote ourselves once more to national tasks. But I must admit: a society that is purely secular, a liberal society that shuns the religious and everything that transcends the individual self, can only repress Auschwitz. Where the ego is supreme, one can only repress guilt. One can absorb, retain, and bear it only together with others.

And so, after this elaborate journey, we arrive at the theme of the two previous texts.

It is the Holocaust, he asserts, that remains the enduring stigma on German national consciousness and thus prevents Germans from expressing themselves in an unconstrained way. Using the subjunctive, he says that if Germans *could* come to terms with Auschwitz (he uses the same term *bewältigen* that he had scorned in his speech of the same year), they could devote themselves to national tasks, the reconstitution of a German national identity. But he suggests that the secularism and individualism of German society make this impossible, leaving repression of guilt as the only possible route. This repression is connected in the pages that follow with the retreat from history, with the writer Beckett and the philosopher Adorno cited as models, and thus from the notion of the *Volk* and from God. It is interesting to note that Walser, who was raised by a mother who was a fervent Catholic but who renounced his faith as an adult, suggests that society needs God, as defined here: "our need to transcend the ego." This national deficit is then connected explicitly to the division of Germany, which is seen here as the primary symptom of the diseased state of German national consciousness.

In the final paragraph he returns to the first person, suggesting ironically that maybe this is all just his personal problem, that everyone else is perfectly content with the current situation in the two Germanys. Stating that he feels the need to overcome the division of Germany, he mockingly points out that many regard this longing as obsolete or old-fashioned, but to him it's just old; in other words, his desire is one that connects him with centuries of German history, in opposition to the short-sighted ahistorical perspective dominant in both Germanys.

Jörg Magenau legitimately points to the problematic concept of the German "Volk," employed by Walser here, as a class-based entity limited essentially to the working class and lower-middle class, one from which intellectuals are excluded. But given Walser's strong identification with his lower-middle-class roots, Magenau asks: "But wouldn't [Walser] himself be the best example of an intellectual who does belong to the *Volk*?"[9] This ambivalence is a key component of Walser's conflicted sense of national identity.

Clearly this speech constitutes a major shift from the two previous texts; here German guilt for the Holocaust is viewed as the problem preventing Germans from devoting themselves to national tasks, rather than as an essential fact that each German must face and deal with. In

---

[9] Magenau, *Martin Walser*, 371.

light of his later criticism of public memorialization of the Holocaust in the Peace Prize speech, it is interesting to note his claim here that it is the current-day cult of individualism that makes it impossible to deal with the Holocaust, and that only as a collective can Germans "absorb, retain, and bear" this guilt. Another issue presents itself in this essay, namely his synecdochal use of "Auschwitz" to represent the Holocaust. The 1965 essay was inspired by the Auschwitz trials, and the 1979 speech was given at an exhibition of drawings from Auschwitz, so in those cases it was not problematic to refer exclusively to Auschwitz. But when dealing with the entire legacy of the Holocaust, as he does here, it might be observed that to refer only to Auschwitz could be understood as minimizing the extent of the genocide committed.

Anyone familiar only with the two previous texts might well think that Walser struggled with the legacy of the Holocaust in a manner and to an extent shared by few of his fellow Germans, and that he thus deserved a place of honor and respect as one of the few Germans to face these painful issues. This essay, without explicitly retracting any of the positions assumed in the two previous texts, introduces us to the more problematic aspects of Walser's more recent texts on the German past and German identity, and to the "literary" devices he uses to wrestle with his conflicted feelings.

Speaking of Germany (A Report) (1988)

Context

THE SPEECH THAT FOLLOWS was delivered at the Kammerspiele Theater in Munich on October 30, 1988, as part of a series called "Reden über unser Land," or "Speeches about Our Country." Though he was not involved in any major controversies in the 1980s, Walser's reputation as a writer who had abandoned his older left-wing convictions in favor of right-leaning nationalist sentiments had established itself among most of his former left-wing colleagues, in spite of the fact that during these years he signed at least one pro-labor petition and spoke enthusiastically about the success of the Green Party in gaining seats in the German Parliament. Still, this "reclassification" was not the material of newspaper headlines or TV news reports and thus did not penetrate into the general public, which continued to purchase and read his novels. This 1988 speech, however, was to provoke a significant public controversy.

In the speech, Walser refers to what was undoubtedly the most significant controversy in West Germany during the 1980s, the so-called "Historikerstreit" or Historians' Debate. This had begun with an article by the conservative historian Ernst Nolte in the *FAZ*, in which he argued that the Holocaust was a response to the class-based mass murders of Stalin's Soviet regime; he thus rejected the notion of the Holocaust as a unique event and suggested that it was essentially a defensive reaction by a German state that felt threatened. His position was attacked by Jürgen Habermas in the progressive news weekly *Die Zeit* (*Time*), who referred to Nolte's essay as an attempt at "Schadensabwicklung," a canceling-out or negating of Nazi crimes. There followed an intense and very public debate, pitting Habermas and other left-leaning historians (including Hans Mommsen, Martin Broszat, and Heinrich August Winkler) against Nolte and his supporters (including Joachim Fest, Andreas Hillgruber, and Klaus Hildebrand). Some historians — including Christian Meier, whom Walser cites as the voice with which he found himself most in sympathy — attempted to find a middle ground, rejecting the attempt to minimize the Holocaust by equating it with other crimes, but suggesting that it was not invalid per se to make comparisons between different totalitarian systems. This controversy attracted considerable attention, both in Germany and abroad, because it was widely viewed as representing not just a quarrel about historical interpretation but also an attempt to "rescue" Germany and the Germans from the stain of Nazi crimes and thus make possible a more positive self-image. Related to this was a phrase used by West German Chancellor Helmut Kohl in his speech to Israel's Knesset in 1984 (the first by a German Chancellor), the "Gnade der späten Geburt" ("the grace of a late birth"); by this he meant that as someone born in 1930 he need feel no guilt for Nazi crimes.[1] This phrase would haunt Kohl a year later during the "Bitburg" controversy, when, as part of ceremonies marking the fortieth anniversary of the end of the Second World War and celebrating the fact that the former enemies were now close allies, Kohl had persuaded President Ronald Reagan to attend a ceremony at a German military cemetery in Bitburg. Only after Reagan had agreed to this did it become widely known that the cemetery contained not only the graves of Wehrmacht (regular army) soldiers but also those of the Waffen-SS, the Nazi elite corps that had been implicated in numerous war crimes. This controversy is significant also because, while the vast majority of Germans felt the ceremony should go forward regardless, the small but growing German Jewish community, which throughout the postwar era had for understandable reasons kept a very low profile in German public life, was vocal in its opposition.

All of these controversies and slogans signaled a new willingness among Germans to embrace their nationality with pride in a way that had been difficult in the previous decades. But beginning in the late 1980s this transformation in German national consciousness was overshadowed by developments in the Soviet Union — Gorbachev's introduction of *perestroika* (economic reorganization) and *glasnost* (openness in public policy), and his pursuit of accommodation with the West. Still, it needs to be remembered that when this speech was held, only one year before the fall of the Berlin Wall in November 1989, the notion of German unification still seemed an unattainable goal to most people. What con-

---

[1] The journalist Günter Gaus subsequently pointed out that he had coined the phrase earlier than Kohl, but he distanced himself from what he saw as Kohl's attempt to put an end to discussions of German guilt.

cerned Walser in this speech, however, was not the practical measures that would lead to this result but an assertion that, contrary to the claims of those both on the left and on the right who viewed West and East Germany as two separate nations, there was still a meaningful element, embodied not only in historical tradition but in the consciousness of an East German poet whom he cites, of what can only be called German national identity.

Martin Walser: Speaking of Germany (A Report) (1988)

C AN ONE, OR IS ONE EVEN OBLIGED to, evaluate the images from one's youth ex post facto, or is one allowed simply to abandon oneself forever to this rich onrush of images? I have the feeling that I can't handle my memories just any way I want. For example, it's not possible for me to instruct my memory with the aid of knowledge I have obtained in the meantime. My memory reaches back into a time that, I have since learned, was frightful. Every face of a party member, every military uniform, every teacher, and all faces seen from a close distance show that they belong to that time. But they don't show the frightfulness itself. A sixteen- or eighteen-year-old who didn't notice the existence of Auschwitz. Childhood and youth unfold their infinite hunger and thirst, and if uniforms, the faces of commanding officers and the like offer themselves to one's consciousness, then it all just gets swallowed. The local party chapter leader appears to me just as he did even then: a pathetic guy croaking with a Bavarian-Franconian accent and wearing a screamingly yellow-brown uniform that never seemed to belong anywhere, neither in the region nor in the season. He looked as if it had cost him all his courage to leave his official's apartment and to step onto the village street. Every additional step must have cost him additional courage. When he finally made it to the meeting site, all he could produce was this half-hearted croaking.

The light in which my memory presents to me objects and people from back then is an abiding light, an element that offers a kind of precision. One didn't know that one would remember it all so precisely. Above all, one didn't know that one would not be able to add anything to these images. No commentary, no explanation, no evaluation. The images are inaccessible to any briefing. Everything I have learned in the years since has not altered these images. When I surround the images with today's standards, it seems to me that the images don't require any special instruction. The knowledge I have acquired about the murderous dictatorship is one thing, my memory is another. To be sure, that's the case only as long as I keep the memory to myself. As soon as I want to share it with someone else, I notice that I cannot convey the innocence of the memory. I don't have the courage, or I don't have the ability, to tell about scenes of work in freight cars filled with coal, because the knowledge that people were transported to concentration camps in the same kind of freight car intrudes. If I wanted to be able to describe these scenes, I would have to transform myself into an anti-fascist child. I would thus have to speak in the way one speaks about those times today. So all that would remain would be a person of today speaking. Just another one speaking about those times as if he were then the person he is today. An embarrassing procedure. For me, at any rate. The past seen from today's vantage point — can there be anything more superfluous? Certainly there can't be anything more misleading. Misleading, if the past is supposed to be portrayed by this means. That's why most depictions of the past are really information about the present. The past provides the material with which one proves one's humanity.

Historians who would proceed in the same way as I would be assigned to the category of Historicism. Not an especially esteemed school at the moment, apparently. But there are still scholars, for instance in England, who bring important insights to light through this method.

I have had to say all this in advance, because Germany for me is a word from that past. I have as much subsequently acquired knowledge about this past as everyone else. The full extent of our crimes. And if it's difficult to explain even how one can keep every scene from one's childhood free from what surrounded that childhood, how is one supposed to explain that one would like still like to rescue a word like "Germany"? To rescue it for further use. At first one of course believes that one can speak about this country, about *our* country, without having to speak about Germany. But history is indispensable. If our history had gone well, I'd go to the theater in Leipzig tonight and I'd be in Dresden tomorrow, and the fact that I'd be in Germany would be of little or no importance. But precisely because it's missing, Thuringia holds me captive with its saints and craftsmen, its toys and cutlery, charcoal burners and forests, with a diversity of structure that reaches into the interior of the earth. When I ride by Magdeburg today in a train, because of my embarrassment and regret I don't even know where I'm supposed to look. And when I think about Königsberg,[2] I fall into a maelstrom that spins me around and devours me. And each time I return, like the fisherman in Edgar Allan Poe's "Descent into the Maelstrom," with hair grown even whiter. The fact that one cannot consent to what has happened gnaws at one. It's because of one's generation. Younger people are free of these

[2] At the time of this essay (1988), the cities of Leipzig, Dresden, and Magdeburg and the state of Thuringia were all part of East Germany; they were all to become part of united Germany three years later. Königsberg, however, the hometown of the philosopher Immanuel Kant, is now called Kaliningrad and remains a Russian enclave on the far side of Poland from Germany.

feelings. What is Hecuba or Königsberg to them? But even contemporaries who are closer to my age are freer of these feelings than I am. This is the experience about which I have to report. That is my problem. For the time being I'm not getting tired of talking about it, in the hope that I'll learn one day that it's not just my problem.

When the conversation is about Germany, one knows from experience that it won't go well. It doesn't matter if I launch into this Germany-conversation alone, in other words into a conversation with myself, or if I try to do it in writing or by conversing with others — every time it turns out badly: I get into conflict with myself and with others. The result is hopelessness. Even a discussion with myself about Germany is painful, because one isn't really alone in this discussion; one's reacting to arguments that have been forced on one by others, which, although they don't suit one, one can't rid oneself of. It's precisely in discussing Germany that one learns that everyone is right. Is there anything one can say about Germany that isn't right? — For me, this experience goes back at least ten years. Even with old acquaintances, almost-friends, every time the conversation ends in frostiness, distance, embarrassment. Gradually it becomes clear to me that each person is working through a different history: his own history, and often that of his whole family as well. Never do I fire off slogans as unstoppably as in a conversation about Germany. But the same is true of those with whom I'm conversing. But who started it? And already our most central text is the debate about war guilt, and my conversation partners have become opponents, and the slogans (which don't even need us as real persons any more) thunder at us in a painfully narrow and totally German space. Perhaps we should console each other with this reflection: anyone who doesn't fall below his usual standard in a conversation like this doesn't have any standards. I'll mention a couple of the statements that regularly aggravate me, in other words, provocative comments: Germany never really existed anyway. In a thousand years, only the few decades between 1870 and 1945. And those were the worst in all of history. Clemenceau had good reason to open the 1919 peace negotiations on January 18, the day on which forty-eight years earlier the so-called German Empire had been founded in Versailles. So — never again may Germany be allowed to exist. Because from German soil . . . Everyone knows this phrase.[3] Without any prospect of impressing those who keep hammering away at this point, I'll quote the Canadian Social Democrat and peace researcher Hans Sinn

[3] A reference to a famous statement by former West German chancellor Willy Brandt: "Never again can a war be allowed to start from German soil."

(1986): "Today there are more weapons of mass destruction in the territory of East and West Germany than anywhere else in the world." And
after all, that is a consequence of our non-sovereignty in both the East
and the West. A consequence of the division of our country. A united
Germany, open to the world in a manner similar to that of Austria or
Switzerland today, could not possibly be worse than these two fragments
of Germany, both teeming with weapons. And in any case wars don't
take place in Europe any more. This isn't an accomplishment; it's simply
the result of precisely those seventy-five years, and of those two last great
wars. In recent times even the hawks on both sides know this. So please,
don't anyone come and say: a less divided Germany, a united Germany
would be a danger to peace. The textbook argument to justify the division, which I've heard from intellectuals on both sides — that there
never really was a Germany, just a bunch of contentious small states —
only explains the map of German history devised by feudal cabinets.
When the universalist idea of an empire, one that still bore the words
"German nation" in its title,[4] breathed its last, an attempt was made by
the *Volk* to bring about a genuine, in other words a national, unification.
To think in terms of a "Fatherland" was a crime in 1848: it meant the
equivalent of being democratic, desiring national unity. The Communist
Party in 1848 formulated it thus: "All Germany is declared to be a united
and indivisible republic." But what was founded in 1871 was not what
had been desired in 1848. Two examples from the everyday historical
reality of Germans. In 1812 the physician Dr. Karl Christian Wolfart of
Berlin wrote, in a journal edited by Heinrich Zschokke in Switzerland,
about the physician Franz Anton Mesmer from the Lake Constance
region, who thirty years earlier had become famous due to the therapy
named after him: "The honor of this great discovery belongs indisputably to Germany, as it was the cradle of its originator." And a Frankfurt
physician wrote, also in 1812, in a letter to Franz Anton Mesmer: "I
cannot avoid telling you of my joy over the demonstration you have
recently received of the great acclaim given to your teachings by the
physicians of Germany and by a German government." *The* physicians of
Germany and *a* German government. This is very precisely expressed,
and thus probably a reliable indicator. Germany existed, despite the fact
that there were several German governments. And so it is again today.
With this difference: back then people wanted the so-called fatherland to

---

[4] A reference to the Holy Roman Empire, which in German is called the "Holy Roman
Empire of the German Nation," since it centered on the German-speaking lands of
Europe.

receive a political formation; today people, or at least the leading spokesmen (the brightest and most clever ones) have made their peace with the punishment of a divided land. To this end, they live with an edited version of German history that serves their current need. At this point in the discussion of Germany people regularly point me to the case of Austria. They ask me if I think that Austria should be incorporated into the German state. I don't. To deepen the well-meaning but simple-minded selection of images from German history that is now predominant, one can point out that the "Provisional National Assembly" that met in Vienna on November 12, 1918 invoked the right of national self-determination proclaimed by President Wilson and adopted a resolution, Article 2 of which began as follows: "German Austria is part of the German Republic." The Social Democrat Karl Renner, the first head of government of democratic Austria, commented at the time: "Article 2 is a commitment." And on March 21, 1919 the Weimar National Assembly adopted the following resolution: "The whole of German Austria will enter into the German Reich as a member state." But as early as September of the same year, Clemenceau saw to it that this attempt at unification was prohibited. Austria had to and was able to become independent. But Austria's gradual process of becoming independent cannot be compared with a division. Division is the opposite of development. What could be built on in Vienna would never be possible in East Berlin. Division is an intervention, an exercise of power, a punitive action. The fact that I refer to the Yalta and Teheran conferences and their consequences as a punitive action leads my conversation partners to raise their eyebrows in disapproval. I hasten to add that we earned this punishment. But surely not forever. The purpose of this punishment, after all, was not atonement but rather resocialization. Don't we feel that we've been resocialized? Neither in East nor in West Germany is there any indication of a reversion to our old ways. People don't believe that Germany could ever be harmless. And in turn, I ask that they show me no pictures of Silesia Day[5] or news reports about some organization of right-wing neurotics. At the same time, it seems to me very unjust to mention the pain felt at the loss of Silesia in the same breath as Neo-Nazism. But if German historical developments could be prevented by such arguments, then the United States of America would have to be confined to an institution, with the diagnosis: racial-religious autism. But

[5] Silesia was part of Germany before 1945 but was transferred to Poland after the war (with a small portion to Czechoslovakia), and most of the large population of ethnic Germans were forcibly expelled. "Silesia Day" was associated with generally right-wing speakers who claimed that this territory still belonged to Germany.

this isn't necessary, because the diagnosis, in spite of all the embarrassing tirades of clannish and TV-preachers, isn't at all accurate. So: if the danger of reversion to old habits no longer exists — and anyone who can't see that is simply denying the last forty years of German history — then there's only one possible motive remaining for the continued division of Germany: the self-interest of other countries. East and West. An interest that decides all, but that may not called by more accurate names. That too is part of the simplistic selection of public opinion that controls us. We nod our heads to anything at all only out of fear that if we don't, people will think we're Nazis. And the outside world acts as if a no-longer-divided Germany would be a danger once more, as it was in the first half of the century. This has been said often enough in all European countries in the last thirty years. It is in the interest of other countries strictly to maintain the division of Germany by means of this pretext. What's grotesque is that within Germany, especially in West Germany, this pretext is fervently repeated. Especially by intellectuals. Many of them think they're progressive when they consider this product of the last war to be reasonable. Depending on their area of expertise, they draw appropriately crocheted blankets of consolation over the gap created by the division: they speak of a "historical nation," a "culture nation," a "sports nation" (by counting up medals during the Olympics). The Swedish daily paper *Dagens Nyheter* posed the following question to East German leader Erich Honecker in 1986: "During the current World Soccer Championship we've noticed that ever since East Germany was eliminated from the competition, people here are rooting for the West German team. Are you rooting for them too, Mr. Honecker, and should we view this as a sign of German solidarity?" Honecker was so constrained, so taken aback, so disconcerted, so tied up in knots, that all he could say was: "I don't believe that. If you're a real soccer fan, than you root for the best team. I don't believe this should be viewed as a political position," and so on.

Probably the compulsion under which such convoluted sentences arise has already been overcome historically. Moscow is no longer so imperialistic that it could press its self-serving demand of internationalism with insensitive power. Estonians, Latvians, and Lithuanians are declaring their own claim to nationhood. But the Germans are still throwing together these convoluted sentences! Why don't we at least suggest to our friends in the West that they imagine what it'd be like to have a border like ours along the Ohio River, along the Loire, or between

Rome and Florence? Maybe this could help an Andreotti[6] imagine what the border along the Elbe is to us. Only if there were a danger that we could become Hitler Germans or Hohenzollern Germans once more would the division be justified, indeed necessary. But to attribute this danger to us Germans today is grotesque.

At this point in the conversation I readily make the mistake of reproaching my opponents with the accusation that they are perpetuating fascism by insisting on anti-fascist posturing. Then of course the Brecht quotation comes to mind, that the womb that that one crawled out of is still fruitful.

I counter: the image is brilliant, because it reflects precisely the circumstances of the first half of the twentieth century. But it's only the first person to say this who was a genius. Then I get served today's version: "The Germans are all Nazis," "Wherever we buy our noodles, it's always just Nazis we encounter." (In this case the quotation is from Austrian dramatist Thomas Bernhard, but it's just as loud and simplistic in the works of the German filmmaker Herbert Achternbusch et al. Almost gratefully we can report that the writer Peter Handke doesn't inflict this kind of thing on us, Botho Strauss and Werner Herzog still less.) Anyone who contradicts this fashionable masturbatory political tone incurs the worst penalty: it's said he can't take a joke. So if we can't take a joke, we must all be Nazis. The market value, to be sure, is enormous, but the face value is minimal. Historians must marvel at this, sooner or later: how many important people, years after the defeat of fascism, refreshed their anger *and* their clear conscience throughout their lives through anti-fascist gestures. If we were "all" still "Nazis," we would actually have to request that the division be maintained. Fortunately, there was the "Historians' Debate."[7] Perhaps there was a bit too much "clear conscience" on one side of the debate. In spite of that, one can be very grateful that Jürgen Habermas "triggered" (as Munich political scientist Kurt Sontheimer put it) this argument.

This controversy revealed a wide range of points of view and judgments. Instead of the couple of clichés that circulated previously, a

[6] Giulio Andreotti served several terms as Prime Minister of Italy in the 1970s, 1980s, and 1990s.

[7] The reference is to the so-called "Historikerstreit" of 1986, in which some conservative West German historians argued that the Holocaust was not unique, in fact that it was arguably a response to similar crimes committed by the Soviet Union. The well-known philosopher Jürgen Habermas initiated the debate by attacking the writings of four of these historians for, as he saw it, pursuing a political agenda, namely attempting to create a more "positive" German national identity.

diversity of opinions. Now, when we speak of Germany, we can make use of these offerings. Now one can sometimes identify with a historian, instead of with athletes. Since they do not reach agreement, at the end of the day we don't know anything for sure, but our uncertainty consists of clearer positions, the contradictions are more sharply etched inside us. I have had an experience relevant to this: the more someone claims to be the only one who knows the truth and above all the only one whose views are justified, the less I can adopt his view of our history. I felt most in sympathy with the views of the historian Christian Meier, and feel that he expressed my opinions the best. But none of these conflicting views were totally alien to me. What raged so polemically in public is as well known to me as my own inner life. The opinions of both Habermas *and* Hillgruber find a comfortable place within me. In order to make the impossibility of my position even clearer: it seems to me that the German question cannot be grasped either from the "Left" or the "Right." I can see already how in the next round of the conversation about Germany in the conservative *FAZ* or the left-wing *konkret* I'll be lumped together with Kaiser Wilhelm II, since (it's said) he wanted to know only Germans.

An example of how our national question is handled among our literary intellectuals:

In the *FAZ* of December 17, 1986 a sentence by German playwright Franz Xaver Kroetz was quoted: "East Germany is as foreign to me as Mongolia." In response, Marcel Reich-Ranicki, who's not exactly famous for being agreeable, wrote: "I like that line very much." And then Kroetz once more: "It's a wise arrangement that we have two Germanys." Because in his view "world peace" is less endangered. So, once again the tritest, most unprovable of all formulas to justify Germany's division. Reich-Ranicki: "All respect for a man who resists the national or nationalistic hypocrisy that's now typical around here with such a declaration." Is this true? Is a "national hypocrisy that sometimes tips over into nationalist hypocrisy" now "typical" "around here"? So much is clear: if East Germany is as foreign to a person "as Mongolia," then that person "pleases" Reich-Ranicki extraordinarily. There's no need for arguments, either someone likes what you have to say or they don't. And this personal liking, which lacks any argumentation, is now furnished with the power of newspapers. Such a sentence says remarkably little, in and of itself. But in the *FAZ* it helps create a mood that favors the division of Germany. The fact that I, as opposed to Kroetz, cannot make my peace with this division is explained by the critic by saying that I have fallen victim to West German "slogans"; "for forty years" the Alemanni and the Swabians have been "far more important" to me than "the question of Germany as a whole." I have thus out of purely opportunistic reasons fallen prey to the newest trends. It's certainly peculiar: instead of an argument, the insinuation of a motive, and of course the worst one possible. So is my interest in Germany an effect of the latest "slogans" from Bonn? In response, I must go back more than a decade and quote from a speech that I gave in the neighborhood of the *FAZ,* in Bergen-Enkheim, on August 30, 1977, and that has been available in print since 1978. In that speech I tried to sum up my feelings as follows: "The fact that these two countries exist is the product of a catastrophe, the causes of which are well known. I find it intolerable to allow German history to end with the product of a catastrophe. . . . If someone from 1955 to 1975 perceived the German problem merely as a consumer of the so-called mass media, then he's waiting today (if he consumed conservative media) in a Gothic Kyffhäuser[8] dome for the iron day of unification, or he's willing, if he's oriented himself to the more liberal media, to sashay around an open wound forever as a drugged pragmatist. I couldn't name a single practical step that might contribute to overcoming the tragi-comical non-relationship between the two Germanys. But I sense an elemental need to be allowed to travel to Saxony and Thuringia under conditions entirely different from those that now exist. Saxony and Thuringia to me are names that resound far into the past and deep into my psyche, and I cannot enter them as losses in our account book. Nietzsche is no foreigner. Leipzig may not be ours at the moment. But Leipzig is mine. I cannot delete Germany from my historical consciousness. They can print new maps, but they can't revise my consciousness. I refuse to take part in the liquidation of history. In me, a different sort of Germany still has a chance. The world wouldn't need to cringe at a Germany of that sort. And yet at the moment this is a pure utopia, a kind of wishful thinking. The process of history is guided by need; in fact, it arises out of need. So it really does depend on us — on all of us. All of us bear the corpse of the fatherland on our back — the beautiful, dirty fatherland that they have cut in two, so that now we have to live in two abbreviated versions. We aren't allowed to want to live in these. We should — I say this trembling at my boldness — give as little recognition to West Germany as we do to East Germany. We must keep open the wound called Germany."

[8] Kyffhäuser is the name of a mountain range in Thuringia (then in East Germany) associated with the tomb of the Holy Roman Emperor Frederick Barbarossa, who in legends was said not to be dead at all but waiting to arise again and restore German national pride.

End of the quotation from 1977. Even a prominent *FAZ* editor can't know everything; in fact he's not allowed to know everything. The less one knows, the more infallible one is. And the Pope is always the most infallible of all.[9] It's interesting to me that my confession — that I couldn't make my peace with the division of Germany — was responded to in 1986 with similar scorn in both *FAZ* and *konkret*. This shows how passé the national theme is, or (to put it in up-to-date terms) how unhip it is. Among the good reasons for this situation are the misuse of the issue by conservatives, and Adenauer's[10] hullabaloo about reunification. On the other hand, Brandt and Bahr at the time of the Basic Treaty[11] both still spoke of the German question's being open. But today Brandt derides the German question as a kind of "schizophrenia" with which we should no longer afflict the rest of the world, and Bahr speaks of "constitutional patriotism." The phrase reeks of the labor of trying to come to terms with a situation, the labor from which it originates. Everything that's offered to us smells like a substitute. And I lack the courage to respond appropriately to the "realism" of Schily,[12] who in order to avoid further hypocritical June 17th demonstrations suggests we delete the preamble to the constitution, which makes Germany our obligation. So we're supposed to keep pretending?! What then do I have to suggest?! The solution, please?!

What is possible always exceeds the calculations of experts. Even before Gorbachev one could say that. Two reasonable people in power at the same time in Washington and Moscow, and no mere custodians in Bonn and East Berlin, and the division shrinks. Since Gorbachev it's easier to say something like that. Since he's been in power the world is less sharply divided. I don't want to get into the business of being a

[9] Marcel Reich-Ranicki, the critic to whom Walser refers, is known as the "Literaturpapst" or "Pope of literature" due to his high media visibility and influence.

[10] Konrad Adenauer was the first chancellor of West Germany from 1949 to 1963.

[11] The "Grundlagenvertrag" of 1972, reached during the chancellorship of Willy Brandt and negotiated by the cabinet officer Egon Bahr, created a basis for relations between East and West Germany for the first time, but the West German government stated at the same time that it did not renounce its commitment to eventual reunification.

[12] Otto Schily, who first attained prominence as a defender of left-wing radicals like Horst Mahler, was elected to Parliament in 1983 as a member of the Green party. He left the Green Party in 1989 and was appointed Minister of the Interior by Gerhard Schröder in 1990. June 17 was the date of the uprising of 1953 in East Germany. The preamble to the German *Grundgesetz* or Basic Law of 1949 claimed that the document spoke for all Germans, including those who were excluded from participating in the process.

Kremlin astrologer and chew over and interpret Gorbachev's latest statements. Whatever he may or must say, the tempest he created, perestroika, will one day reach East Germany, and then the political language there will cast off its pseudo-religious filters, and Germans will be able to understand each other once more. Even now we can imagine a time in which the hostility between Adenauer and Ulbricht[13] will be regarded with the same shake of the head with which for a long time now we've regarded the grotesque conflicts between Catholics and Protestants. As early as 1966, in the journal *Kursbuch* (Timetable), Hans Magnus Enzensberger[14] called the problem of Germany an "anachronism," and wrote that it was "an especially complex and protracted and outdated dispute from the time of the Cold War." Enzensberger at that time made suggestions that were more positive and full of historical imagination than anyone else's; he recommended that we treat East Germany with respect, because this would make "agreement or even unification" more likely. He wants to create a confederation of the two Germanys, and from that allow a "German Council" to arise in which delegates of the West and East German parliaments would work together. In Article 61 of his *Catechism on the German Question* he asks himself what repercussions his suggestions would have on the "social orders in Germany," and answers: "They would lose their insularity; they would have to learn from each other; they could offer each other versions of their future." Unfortunately, neither of the two German railroads took note of this timetable. And yet it was not written in vain. What can still please us in this "catechism" is that an intellectual deals with our problem as if it were essential for him to solve it. One sentence at the end of his work, which one could call a trophy of precision, shows what happens to one when one deals with the German question: ". . . what is necessary seems identical to what is impossible." Doesn't this remind one of the Mecklenburgian steadfastness with which Uwe Johnson[15] insisted until recently that with his move from East to West Germany he had not changed his country but only his place of residence!

But since Enzensberger's catechism and Johnson's declaration, the power of the Cold War to thwart positive initiatives has so exhausted

[13] Walter Ulbricht was the leader of East Germany from 1953 to 1971.

[14] Hans Magnus Enzensberger is one of the leading poets of postwar Germany; the journal *Kursbuch* or "Timetable," which he founded in 1965, was a leading voice of the left-wing movement of the 1960s and 1970s.

[15] Uwe Johnson, a prominent German writer especially known for his novel *Mutmassungen über Jakob* (*Speculations about Jacob*, 1959), left East Germany for the West in 1959.

itself that, almost unexpectedly, we are closer to achieving peace than ever before.

Perhaps there was a kind of logic in the fact that the war that ended in 1945 has remained until now without a peace treaty. We can do without a peace à la Versailles or Yalta. Perhaps this time peace will be sealed when those who seal it have really become peaceable. And even those who until now have regarded the division of Germany as a prerequisite for peace would have to admit that in this case the division would no longer be necessary. What matters now is that we feel that the division has no validity for the future. For the time being that would be enough of a "solution." Politicians, educators, the mass media — thus all the public spokesmen — have done much, with sharply varying motives, to make the division seem reasonable to us.

Left- and right-wing intellectuals among us probably agree about few things as much as they do about this proposition: the division of Germany is acceptable. The successful West German citizen doesn't want his hard-earned standard of living — and also his democratic standards — reduced to the level of today's Magdeburg. That's understandable. The question I fear most in discussions about Germany is: what's your problem? Because the lack I want to express is evidently hard to make understandable, I evade the question by pointing to what others are lacking. I quote what Eduard Vogelsang, who emigrated from Poland to East Germany, wrote in the *FAZ* (and not in the literature section): "In spite of her giving up the German language, my mother, a woman with a strong German consciousness, conveyed this feeling to me as well. But probably signs of a psychic split have remained. The Germans who for whatever reasons remained in the formerly German territories of Eastern Europe paid a high price for it: they paid with the loss of their mother tongue, and not seldom (those of the younger generation) the loss of their national identity."

Then I'll pull out another letter right away and quote what was written to my neighbor Ricarda from a friend in Dresden: "Now please don't be annoyed if I've groused a bit, but there's no avoiding it. But to make life here comprehensible to you won't be possible anyway, the difference is too huge. I just hope that through my grousing I have made you glad that when Germany was divided your families lived on the right side! It makes me very happy that you won't forget me . . ."

With these examples I aim to prove that Germans still exist. This needs to be proved, because in the discussion about Germany the examples of Carthage and the Aztecs[16] are held up to one's face. And when I maintain that there are still Germans, I'm not thinking of any flag-waving or national hymns. I do know how little importance the successful West German accords his passport. He is at least a European. Still, he has to figure that in Paris he'll meet mainly Frenchmen, in London English people, and in Rome Italians. Then what is he? It's precisely when one is abroad that one learns that one is a German. Even Metternich, in a conversation with Napoleon in 1813, openly identified himself as a German. Today being reminded abroad that one is a German always saddens rather than pleases us. But if one in chic fashion powdered over the German shadow that one casts, who would one be?

They say that in the last thirty years it has often happened that Germans abroad have made an unpleasantly German impression precisely by trying to be accommodatingly un-German.

There is still a quality of Germanness, which people abroad would call "German to the bone,"[17] that is worthy of the same respect given to its French, Polish, or Italian equivalents. For example, there is a German language, a German literary tradition that was not discredited between 1933 and 1945 and that was not dissolved into the international tradition after 1945. At this point, I'd like to share a reading experience. The author: Wulf Kirsten, born 1934 in Klipphausen in the district of Meissen, now lives and works in Weimar. His poetry collection *The Earth at Meissen* is now available even in the West (Frankfurt, 1987). This excerpt comes from the poem "the earth at Meissen":

> down to the Elbe wind
> with green scales the feathered valleys like the edges of shafts.
> grit mills, the forest hermits, along the gravel gullies
> grandfatherly in appearance, play hide and seek in their leafy
>   hollows.
> crouched among the onion-like shale the parish towns.
> to the side, piled up by the blackthorn hedge, the stinky ones:
>   silos filled with turnips.
> behind barns in the field, straw huts covered with foam.
> with shaggy-haired manes the field paths hobble out into the
>   turnip fields.

[16] I.e., civilizations that long ago ceased to exist.

[17] Walser uses the English phrase here.

SPEAKING OF GERMANY: A REPORT (1988)   🐦   71

A poem about winter starts this way:

> the houses cower uncommunicatively
> in buttoned-up hoods
> before their own shadows.

A poem called "little traveled" begins as follows:

> cool from the river valleys the evening scents come before
>   the house
> the seasons of the year fall from the backrests of hills
> like hearty greetings from one's relations,
> the most reliable chronology.

In the poem "at work" the following lines appear:

> gleaning and threshing the oat clips
> setting up and hammering a block of stone,
>
> stacking up a cartload of hay, sending off the animals
> knitting up a fragile pot with wire,
> beating cabbage, peeling turnips,
> putting on tires, boarding up a fence, . . .

The last couplet of this poem:

> propping up a ladder, chopping oat straw,
> confusing the temporal with the eternal.

Kirsten's language is heavy with the past. A language in which one can find resources to protect oneself from haste, accommodation, and loss. Any poem by Kirsten makes it blatantly clear to any West German reader: this wasn't written by one of us. His life is not grounded in judgments, ideas, media-generated apocalypse. He is grounded in objects in his immediate vicinity. He lives as if barefoot. He experiences life with his hands and feet. He doesn't know anything that he hasn't experienced personally. The consequence of this is that his language doesn't make judgments. It drags up objects. To combat forgetting. The languages of our writers and poets in the West, compared with Kirsten's, are addicted to making judgments or statements. What is done is simply to make judgments about everything. That's what we do. And judgments are about all that get made. Objects are seldom mentioned. Nothing is preserved. When I read Wulf Kirsten, I sense what we in West Germany have lost — we writers and we readers. Doesn't much of our literature, compared to Kirsten, seem like pure ideology? I think: our sentences tell us what they intend to say more clearly than they say it. This is, I maintain now a bit hastily, the influence of the opinion-makers on literature. They prefer above all to praise or condemn those writings that do what they themselves do: create opinions à la "German are all Nazis."

You can't do anything with a sentence from a poem by Kirsten. The opinion-content of a sentence by Kirsten is close to zero. *Opinion* is what you may probably call the content that is represented in a sentence by the will of the writer rather than by anything connected to an object.

Kirsten's books have appeared in East Germany with Aufbau Press in Berlin and Weimar and with Reclam in Leipzig. His brilliant description, "The Battle of Kesselsdorf,"[18] is grounded in its empathy with what was suffered. For Kirsten, history dissolves into a chasm between the commanders and those they command. Even his "small town picture" *Kleewunsch* is grounded in this sense of sight that nothing can deceive. I haven't met any intellectual in West Germany for whom the claim to democracy comprises and rules his entire sensibility. In Kirsten's sentences one can't separate the poetic at all from the political capacity to experience reality. An East German accomplishment? Or: just this Wulf Kirsten?

The story of the market town of Kleewunsch is narrated up to the time in which the industry of opinion-creation is developed. From this time onward the writer falls silent about his historical location. He turns to the *district*[19] quite generally and quite concretely: "on the intermingled bushes of the path edges." I have the impression that Wulf Kirsten as a citizen of East Germany has a sense of history that we lack. It's not about assigning guilt; it's about taking stock. Let's take leave of the German poet Kirsten with a few lines from his poem "over seven field margins":

> and a rough-hewn lead dog
> without fuss drags
> the blinded aura of poverty
> to the marketplace.
> above the heights of the Elbe
> the day is crowned.

---

[18] Refers to a battle fought in 1745 near Dresden between the armies of Prussia on one side and Austria and Saxony on the other.

[19] He uses the archaic term "Sprengel," which today is used mainly to designate a church parish or diocese.

I think that we in the West are missing out on something that those in the East can experience. One would need the power of Hölderlin's historical tone to grasp what is transpiring among us Germans at present. In order at least to awaken our sense of loss from its self-forgetting slumber. So that we might seem less possible to ourselves. More dependent on others. Not so much in the right.

What these quotes from Kirsten are intended to evoke is not the form of compensation called "culture nation" but rather the feeling that there is still such a thing as an element of Germanness that is not disgraced. PRIOR to literature. Serving as its basis. Otherwise a Wulf Kirsten couldn't exist. That is a feeling. It is put into words here as an invitation to try it once this way, too. As a feeling. Feeling the language of Kirsten. And it could be that out of this will grow an experience; and the next time when (unavoidably) the conversation revolves around Germany, perhaps this experience will come to mind.

A discussion about Germany would turn out best if one could do without negation. Does one, as long as one is negating what someone else has said, really have anything to say? It's enough just to say what it is that bears us along: the past. What else, if you please? Every tree you see is related to an earlier one. Even what is most fleeting, today's weather, would be nothing if it did not recall the weather of earlier days. And how much more is this the case with houses, thoughts, railroads, dreams, policemen, head coverings, national boundaries. . . . Sometimes nothing remains of a feeling of our present existence because of the onrush of the past. Thread or fabric, word or text — everything is made of nothing but history. The present is nothing but the (temporarily) last moment of history. The tiniest moment of all. But it is also the one that matters and the one that everything boils down to. But without all of history it is really nothing, or even, nothing at all. Every apple that I eat has a name. One may regret this. But it's the way it is. I don't know my way around the consciousness of mayflies,[20] but I assume that every movement of such a creature is determined by its entire history. What is the tip of an iceberg compared to the tip of time! The nation is the mightiest historical occurrence by human measure up to the present moment. *Mighty* in a geological, not a political sense. The nation will surely dissolve itself sooner or later. But not through a division. Not through Yalta-Churchill-Roosevelt-Stalin. What follows from such a compass error is much that is current, but nothing that is decisive.

[20] The German "Eintagsfliegen" literally means "One-day flies."

This is the feeling that is incapable of proving anything but that still cannot be dismissed. In case something of the sort may really exist, a feeling of history. Finally you can't do much more than to prove that it exists. But you can do that. A feeling also can't be prescribed to others. Either you have it or you don't. But if you have it, you *can* admit that you have it: the feeling of history. I hereby state that I have admitted to this.

If everyone else had a blatantly different feeling of history, then one would have to feel somewhat lost. The majority of public spokesmen, on the left and on the right, are co-workers in trying to make the division of Germany seem reasonable. The preamble to the Basic Law and other institutional statements do not constitute an enlivening society. And people aren't being asked. The *Volk*! You're disdainfully called a populist if you think that the German question can only be answered by the *Volk*. One vote in East Germany, one vote among us. Internationally supervised. People's right of self-determination put into practice. It'd be so simple. And equally impossible and unthinkable. We still live in an age where speech occurs only from above to below. From below to above the voice of the *Volk* can be heard only as distorted by public opinion research. Led by this sense of history, one would like to say that the Germans in their two states would, if they could, vote for a path leading to unity. Based on everything we hear from abroad, such a likelihood is enough to prevent any such vote from taking place. So everything depends on the governments. And thus the worst possible scenario. Unless the two German populations did not resign themselves to this pragmatism forever. Thus there's not the slightest concrete prospect of beginning to overcome the division. Accordingly Germany remains a word that's useful at least for weather reports. I myself marvel at the fact that this lack of any concrete prospect of fulfillment does not turn into hopelessness within me. Maybe it's that feeling of history at work.

Commentary

I N THIS SPEECH, WALSER SPEAKS in the first person (in contrast to "Our Auschwitz" and "No End to Auschwitz") but does not resort to the fictionalized third person, as he did in "Handshake with Ghosts" and as he was to do again in the famous Peace Prize Speech. It is worth noting that in this speech he chooses a mode of presentation that in no way denies the personal element. His main point throughout — namely, that in spite of the forty years of division there remains a German national consciousness that is shared by those in the East and in the West, and that this consciousness has substantive historical roots — is one that he presents as a deeply held personal feeling, but one that is shared by Germans in the past and present.

Interestingly, he begins the speech by describing precisely what he was to attempt ten years later in his partly autobiographical novel *Ein springender Brunnen* (A Springing Fountain, 1998), namely to present the memories of a young boy growing up during the Nazi period without superimposing knowledge that was gained subsequently: "A sixteen- or eighteen-year old who didn't notice the existence of Auschwitz." But what might seem at first glance to be a point of literary technique becomes a critique of the general tendency to view the past through the prism of the present.

He then makes the transition to the discussion of Germany, which he labels "a word from that past." Just as he had used the word "Volk" in "Handshake with Ghosts" as a deliberate provocation, here he suggests that to use the term "Germany" at the present time is similarly provocative, since due to the East/West division the common view is that there is no such thing as "Germany." He speaks of how difficult it is to talk about Germany, how every time he attempts to do so he gets into an argument, even within himself. He cites the often-heard argument that Germany hardly existed historically, only between 1871 and 1945, which were arguably the worst years in German history (culminating in two calamitous World Wars), and reports that these conversations inevitably revolve around guilt for Nazi crimes. But then he proceeds to question the premise that the division of Germany contributes to world peace, citing a Canadian scholar who points out that the two Germanys between them have more weapons of mass destruction than any other place in the world. Since the division of Germany can hardly be said to advance the cause of peace, Walser asks, what can possibly justify it? He maintains — not unreasonably — that over the more than forty years since the end of the war, both Germanys have clearly evolved into states that pose no threat to world peace.

Delving into the German past, Walser points out that the German revolutionaries of 1848 aspired to a united Germany that would be a liberal democracy, thus arguing that there is nothing inherently totalitarian about the idea of a united Germany. He cites letters from two physicians writing in 1812, at a time when there were numerous German states, talking about Germany as their nation; from this, he argues that the notion of Germany does not presuppose a single German state, and that since this was the case in 1812, it would hold equally true in 1988. What then, his conversational partners would ask him, would you say about Austria — should it too be part of a divided Germany? Here Walser anticipates one of the more difficult challenges to the idea of a united Germany, since there was widespread sentiment in Austria, after the breakup of the Habsburg Empire and even earlier, for a union with Germany, and, as he points out, this Austrian decision to merge with Germany after the First World War was forbidden by the French prime minister, Clemenceau; thus it might be argued that this should no more be accepted than the post-Second World War division of Germany. To this Walser replies that Austria underwent a process of development leading to independence, and this development cannot be compared with the forcible division of a Germany that had been united. (Interestingly, he does not refer to the "interruption" in Austrian independence brought about by the Nazi annexation of Austria in 1938, which endured until 1945.)

Though he does not deny that Germany after 1945 deserved punishment, he argues that that punishment should not last forever, and denies that there is any rationale for the division other than punishment — once again, he scoffs at the notion that Germany poses a danger to the world. He then argues further that Germans will not point out this obvious reality for fear of being labeled Nazis, and suggests that the only reason for the continued division is "the self-interest of other countries." It is worth noting that he specifies neither which countries are responsible nor how the division of Germany serves their self-interest. But, he argues further, not only do German intellectuals fail to protest against this, they even feel it necessary to endorse this stance, speaking of Germany at most as a "cultural nation." He refers to East German president Erich Honecker's loss for words when confronted with the observation that once East Germany had been eliminated from the World Cup in Soccer, East Germans were rooting for the West German team.

Just as he had targeted German intellectuals for criticism in the essay "Handshake with Ghosts," here he accuses them of "perpetuating fascism" precisely through their "anti-fascist posturing," including even statements like "The Germans are all Nazis." He turns to the Historians' Debate, which he views overall as a healthy opening up of discussion about the German past and German identity. As in the earlier essay, he espouses the virtue of contradiction — he points out that all voices in the debate resonated within him in some way, and states that in his view "the German question cannot be grasped either from the 'Left' or from the 'Right.'"

As an example of "how our national question is handled among our literary intellectuals," Walser quotes a statement by a German writer: "East Germany is as foreign to me as Mongolia," a statement that the critic Marcel Reich-Ranicki then applauds. Since Reich-Ranicki — who comes from a Polish Jewish background, was in the Warsaw Ghetto, and lost most of his family in the Holocaust — was later the apparent target of his 2002 novel *Tod eines Kritikers* (Death of a Critic), Walser's comments here are obviously of interest. It's not unreasonable to say of Reich-Ranicki that he's "not exactly famous for being agreeable" — he published a collection of his reviews under the title *Lauter Verrisse* (Nothing but Bad Reviews), and had given a fair share of bad reviews to Walser's novels — but it's interesting to note that Reich-Ranicki is cited by Walser here as representing the power of the media. Walser was not alone in this view; to this day Reich-Ranicki is known as the "Literaturpapst" (Pope of Literature) in view of his tremendous influence, not only through his reviews in *Die Zeit* and the *FAZ* but also and especially through his popular TV show *Literarisches Quartett* (Literary Quartet), which aired from 1988 to 2002. Still, it is fair to say that most German authors and intellectuals have been somewhat reticent in their public statements about Reich-Ranicki, in light of his Jewish background; Walser, by contrast, appears even in 1988 to thumb his nose at such restraint. Reich-Ranicki here is emblematic for the insidious power of the media in shaping collective consciousness.

In contrast to those (like Reich-Ranicki) who mock Walser's "interest in Germany" as a new kind of political slogan, he quotes from his 1977 Bergen-Enkheim speech to show that the issue has preoccupied him for some time. He also points out that even Willy Brandt's opening of a dialogue with East Germany was accompanied by assurances that West Germany had not abandoned its constitutional commitment to eventual unification, though adding that Brandt had since changed his tune and now derided the desire for unification as "schizophrenia." In the face of a public opinion that has systematically been brought to regard the hope for unification as passé, Walser points out the laboriousness of the discourse that seeks to shelve the idea of unification, using terms such as "constitutional patriotism." Recalling the writer Hans Magnus Enzensberger's comments in 1966 speculating on a possible path to unification, he points out that with Gorbachev in power in the Soviet Union, such a path is more possible than it was when Enzensberger wrote.

Once again, he quotes from letters, this time from contemporary ones, attesting to the feeling of a German national identity, and argues from them that "there is still a quality of Germanness . . . that is worthy of the same respect given to its French, Polish, or Italian equivalents." To illustrate, he quotes from several poems by the East German poet Wulf Kirsten that display this quality of Germanness, a sense of down-to-earth immediacy, one that can (he asserts) never be heard in West Germany, since West German writers are "addicted to making judgments or statements." He closes by once more insisting on the primacy of history in shaping reality, including national consciousness.

*   *   *

Walser's opening comments about experiencing one's memories of the past without superimposing subsequent knowledge, though referring to a child growing up in Nazi Germany, are applicable to this speech as well; it is hard to read the speech today unaffected by the knowledge that what Walser presented (and what was viewed by most) as only a dream — German unification — was to become a reality within months after the speech. His comment "Leipzig may not be ours at the moment. But Leipzig is mine" was confirmed in October of the following year by demonstrators in Leipzig bearing signs that said "Wir sind ein Volk" — "We are one people." Thus it can be argued that Walser was prophetic in his speech, and that he was much more in touch with the realities of the situation than most of his contemporaries.

But once again there are some troubling moments. His answer to the question of whether the logic of his argument would not suggest that Austria be incorporated into a united Germany is not persuasive. Had he focused on the post-1945 period, it could be argued that Austria did then choose an independent path, partly to avoid having to share in the guilt and reparations assigned to West Germany. But he focuses on the post-1918 period, in which Austria (by his account) was forced against its declared wish to become independent, a wish that was still manifest in 1938 when most Austrians welcomed annexation by Nazi Germany.

An even more disturbing element is his repeated accusation that only the "self-interest of other countries" is responsible for maintaining the division of Germany. The fact that he doesn't name the countries he feels are responsible — whether he means the Soviet Union, the United States, Western European countries, or all of the above — is very problematic, evoking something approaching a sense of German paranoia that will be even more pronounced in the Peace Prize Speech.

His derogatory reference to Marcel Reich-Ranicki is problematic for the reasons indicated above. On the other hand, it could also be argued that to take Reich-Ranicki as an emblematic figure representing the all-powerful German cultural media is to acknowledge at least that he is German; there is no reference to his Jewishness in this speech at least.

Although this speech does not display in concrete terms any new position regarding the issue of German unification in comparison with what he had said ten years earlier, it created much more of a public scandal. Walser's biographer Jörg Magenau speculates that this is due in part to the Historians' Debate, which brought issues of German national consciousness to the fore, but even more to the awareness that changes in the Soviet Union under Gorbachev were making thinkable what ten years earlier had seemed only fantasy.[21] He was attacked in *Die Zeit* by the Jewish writer Jurek Becker, a Holocaust survivor who had emigrated from East to West Germany in 1977. Becker rightly took issue with Walser's accusation that the division of Germany was due to foreign interests, and criticized his notion of history without the perspective of the present. Here too, though, it could be argued that Walser was prescient of coming trends, with the increasing popularity of *Alltags-geschichte* or the history of everyday life among German and other historians in the 1980s and 1990s. In any event, Becker's attacks served to strengthen the perception that Walser had changed sides politically, a perception that was fuelled by his acceptance that same year of an invitation to participate in an event sponsored by the Christian Socialist Union, the Bavarian sister-party of the conservative Christian Democratic Union. For many if not most intellectuals, then, Walser was regarded prior to the events of 1989 as someone who had abandoned his left-wing roots and assumed a troubling nationalist stance.

---

[21] Jörg Magenau, *Martin Walser: Eine Biographie* (Reinbek bei Hamburg: Rowohlt, 2005), 413–14.

Experiences while Composing a Sunday Speech: The Peace Prize Speech (1998)

Context

A S IS NOW WELL KNOWN, what seemed a pipe dream at the time of Walser's 1988 speech — the idea of overcoming the division of Germany — was to become a reality within months afterward. In the same year, the East German government felt so threatened by Gorbachev's liberalizing tendencies that it actually forbade the distribution of some Soviet publications it regarded as subversive. In the summer of 1989, the reformist Hungarian regime opened its border with Austria, thus creating a route to the West for citizens of East Germany. East Germans looking to escape also sought asylum in the West German embassies in Czechoslovakia and Poland. In September, West German foreign minister Genscher granted them permission to enter West Germany. Demonstrators in the streets of Leipzig and other East German cities demanded radical reforms, under the slogan "Wir sind das Volk" (We are the people). In a decisive turn, this demand for self-determination, with the change of one word, became a demand for unification: "Wir sind ein Volk" (We are one people). On November 9, a weakened East German government opened the Berlin wall, leading to a celebration by Berliners on both sides of the Wall. A week later, East Germany's hard-line chancellor Krenz was replaced by the reformist Hans Modrow, who promised free elections. When these elections took place in March 1990, the East German ruling party, the SED (Sozialistische Einheitspartei, or Socialist Unity Party), which had renamed itself the PDS (Partei des Demokratischen Sozialismus, or Party of Democratic Socialism), was trounced by the East German branch of the CDU (Christlich-Demokratische Union, or Christian-Democratic Union), the ruling party in West Germany. The new CDU government began negotiations on unification with the West German government of Helmut Kohl. In July, the last barrier to unification was removed when Gorbachev withdrew his objection to a united Germany's remaining in NATO (his agreement was secured by a promise of substantial financial aid to the Soviet Union). The treaty of unification was ratified by the East and West German parliaments in September, and German unification became official on October 3, 1990.

One might suppose that Walser would have felt totally vindicated and at peace as a result of this turn of events. Nevertheless, things were not so simple. The circumstances leading to unification amounted to a collapse of the East German state and its absorption into West Germany. In contrast, it may be recalled that Walser in his 1979 Bergen-Enkheim speech, the one in which he first publicly stated his unwillingness to accept Germany's division, had said "we ought . . . to grant as little recognition to West Germany as we do to East Germany." Though he had in the public view been reclassified as a right-wing conservative, he had throughout his novelistic career displayed a critical view of the market economy dominating the West and its impact on the lives of individuals, and even the essays of the seventies and eighties showed that he had not entirely abandoned the Marxist worldview that he had embraced in the sixties. Thus it is not surprising that even Walser was not pleased at the total dissolution of East Germany and its socialist order and the apparent triumph of the capitalist West. Other German intellectuals, notably the writer Günter Grass, openly opposed unification. In addition, in the first years after unification (the early 1990s) there were several displays of xenophobic violence directed against Turks and other foreigners, as well as some antisemitic acts of desecration and violence, all of which brought old stereotypes about German racism back into world perceptions and into the rhetoric of left-wing intellectuals. It may be remembered that Walser in his 1988 speech argued that the world had nothing more to fear from a united Germany, that Germany had "learned its lesson" after the Nazi years and was now a society like any other. These instances of xenophobia thus gave ammunition to those inside and outside Germany who continued to view Germany as a sick or dangerous culture. As will be apparent from the speech, Walser reacted with impatience bordering on anger to those who saw these violent incidents as symptomatic of broader issues within German society and culture.

Along with these public developments, Walser's critical attitude to the mass media, which was apparent as early as his 1965 essay, was to grow into open hostility after several unpleasant encounters, notably his appearance in February 1989 on the talk show "Freitagnacht" (Friday Night) in which he was attacked by guests from both West and East Germany for his stance on Germany's division, and a broadcast in June

1993 of the TV show "Kulturreport" (Culture Report), in which journalist Tilman Jens attacked Walser, juxtaposing Walser quotations taken
out of context with pictures of acts of right-wing violence, implying that
he was feeding these elements in society with his essays and speeches.
Walser responded to this attack with an article in *Der Spiegel* in which he
suggested that it was the hopelessness caused by the failure of socialism
that was feeding these tendencies in the former East. Associated with his
hostility to the media, especially in the wake of his controversial statements regarding German national identity, was his growing impatience
with the pressure exerted by what he himself referred to by the English
term "political correctness," not only on his speeches, essays, and articles,
but even on his literary work; his novel *Finks Krieg* (Fink's War), which
was to appear in 1996, contained references to Ignatz Bubis that his
Suhrkamp editor, Siegfried Unseld, urged him to delete. Another incident, referred to in the Peace Prize speech, was his speech in honor of
Viktor Klemperer, the Jewish-born scholar and author whose diaries of
his experiences during the Nazi years were published in 1995, thanks in
large part to Walser's efforts. Walser used the occasion to insist that the
catastrophic culmination of the German-Jewish encounter was a result of
the trauma of 1918, and not an inevitability, as many were claiming. This
led to his final break with Jürgen Habermas, who accused him of emphasizing Klemperer's attachment to Germany and underplaying the
horrendous reality of what Germans did to Jews during the Nazi years.
Finally, his 1998 autobiographical novel *Ein springender Brunnen* (A
Springing Fountain), which told of a boy growing up (as had Walser) in
a small town in Germany during the Nazi years, but without any reference to the Holocaust, though it was a great success with the reading
public, was attacked on Reich-Ranicki's TV show *Literarisches Quartett*
(Literary Quartet) for not mentioning Auschwitz.

Another issue that had been debated for almost ten years, but which
came to the fore in the same year (1998), was the planned Holocaust
Monument near the Bundestag (Parliament Building) in Berlin. Even
prior to the Peace Prize speech, Walser had expressed his opposition to
the idea of locating this gigantic memorial in the center of Germany's
capital city. That same year, the Social Democrat Gerhard Schröder replaced the Christian Democrat Helmut Kohl as chancellor. Schröder was
even more outspoken than his predecessor in emphasizing the "normality" of German society, and given that he belonged to a nominally
left-wing party, this plea for normality was thus freed from its associations with right-wing revisionism. Schröder's position vis-à-vis the Berlin
Monument was to wish for a monument "that people want to visit."

Walser's biographer Jörg Magenau speculates that Schröder's affirmation of German "normality" created the context for Walser's speech.

All these factors were to play a role in the text that follows, the notorious acceptance speech he gave upon receiving the prestigious "Peace Prize of the German Book Trade."

Martin Walser: Experiences while Composing a Sunday Speech (1998)

ONCE THE MEDIA HAD ANNOUNCED who was to receive the Peace Prize of the German Book Trade this year, congratulatory messages whirled in. Two adjectives appeared strikingly often in the message texts. The joy of those congratulating was frequently called "boundless." Also, many said that they were eager to hear the speech that the prizewinner would give, it would surely be a critical one. The fact that so many are boundlessly happy because something nice is happening to someone else proves that the capacity for friendliness still lives among us. About the fact that a critical speech was expected from him, the prizewinner could not be equally happy. It was clear: people expected a "Sunday speech" from him, a critical sermon. He was to haul someone, maybe even everyone, over the coals. But after all (he said to himself), you've given this speech before. So give it again, for God's sake. A speech fed by bad news (which is always at hand), which (if one applies some putty to cover up holes in one's argument) can be made so polemically sharp that the media can keep it echoing for two or even two and a half days after.

The prizewinner felt hemmed in, tied down. You see, when he heard about the honor, he had been overcome first by a simple feeling that, put into words, might be stated as follows: he'll say nothing but beautiful things for twenty-five or even thirty minutes — that is, agreeable, lively remarks, suitable for a peace prize. For example he'd praise trees, with which he's been acquainted for a long time through casual contemplation. And then right away the compulsion to justify himself: it's no longer a crime to talk about trees, because in the meantime so many of them have gotten sick.[1] [He could also pose as an expert on sunsets and report that the sun, when it sets over the water, tends to exaggerate.][2] Twenty-five minutes of beautiful things — even if you have to wring it or coax it out of your language — and then you're done. A podium for the Sunday speaker, St. Paul's Church, the most public of occasions, a media presence — and you say only beautiful things! No, it was clear to the

[1] The reference is to the famous lines from Brecht's poem "To Those Born After": "What times are these when / A conversation about trees is almost a crime / Because it entails silence about so many wrongs." (Translation by Walter Kaufmann.)

[2] Several passages that were not part of the speech delivered in St. Paul's Church were included in the print version of the speech; those passages have been placed in square brackets to distinguish them.

prizewinner even without help from the outside, that was not going to work. But then, when he was told explicitly that he was expected to give a critical sermon, his freedom-loving soul rebelled once more. It was clear to me too that I would have to justify my potpourri of the beautiful. The best way to do it would be with confessions like these: I close my eyes to evils to whose elimination I cannot contribute. I have had to learn to look away. I have several corners where I take refuge, into which my glance immediately flees, when the TV screen presents the world to me as unbearable. I find that my reaction is an appropriate one. I don't have to bear what can't be borne. I'm also skilled at thinking about something else. [I cannot go along with the disqualifying of repression. Freud counsels us to replace repression with condemnation. But as far as I can see, his work of enlightenment is directed, not at the behavior of the individual as one's contemporary, but at the person who is shaken to the core by his own instinctual destiny.] I wouldn't be able to get through the day, to say nothing of the night, without looking away and thinking about something else. I am also of the opinion that not everything must be atoned for. I couldn't live in a world in which everything had to be atoned for.

Thus, I admit, it is quite distressing to me when the newspaper reports that an idealist, a veteran of the 1960s who later spied for East Germany and who, by means of NATO documents that he took from Brussels and revealed to East Berlin and Moscow, helped make those in the East understand how little they had to fear a nuclear first strike from NATO — this starry-eyed socialist idealist after unification is sentenced to twelve years in prison and a fine of $60,000, even though the district court in Düsseldorf conceded in its judgment that "he was also concerned with making the intentions of NATO transparent for the sake of removing prejudices and fears on the part of the Warsaw Pact, and thereby contributing to peace. . . ." And it was said he "also did not work for his taskmasters in the East for the sake of money." Wolfgang Schäuble and other Christian Democratic politicians pleaded for amnesty for espionage on both sides as part of the German unification agreement. In spite of this, a law was passed in 1992 that declared the spies of the West blameless and even compensated them for their efforts, but laid the spies of the East open to prosecution. Perhaps I would have been able to distract myself from this event as well, if it did not resemble rather exactly the case that I had portrayed in a novella during the time of Germany's division.[3] When reality imitates fiction to such an extent, an

---

[3] *Dorle und Wolf* (1987).

author can't act as if it didn't concern him any more. If the wretched division of our country were still in place, if the Cold War were still allowed to perpetuate its dangerous nonsense, this prisoner, who is known as "the master spy of the Warsaw Pact at NATO Headquarters in Brussels," would long since have been exchanged for someone of the same importance whom they had imprisoned on the other side. So this prisoner is paying for German unification. Resocialization can't possibly be the goal of this punishment, nor can deterrence. Only atonement remains as an explanation. Our greatly honored federal president has refused to pardon this prisoner. And our president is a jurist of the highest caliber. [I, on the other hand, am a layman. Five years of his twelve-year sentence have already been served. The refusal to grant his claim to a NATO pension, which he has earned through paying contributions, is harsh enough.] Even if the legal-political wheelers and dealers didn't want East and West to be placed on the same level legally, probably because that would have meant a recognition of the East German state after the fact — and so what if it did? — even if the law proves incapable of grasping the happy political turn of events in a human fashion, why should mercy not come before justice? Or so the layman thinks. So after all he can devote his Sunday sermon to a severe presentation of justice in the Federal Republic? But then the speech will be over, I go and eat, and tomorrow I continue working on my next novel, and the spy keeps on atoning, into the next millennium. If that is not a painfully embarrassing thought, then what is? But is this foreseeable ineffectuality a reason not to do something you should do? Or must you avoid giving a critical speech precisely because the only reason you speak of this punishment, which you feel to be senseless and unjust, is because you're supposed to give a critical Sunday sermon? Normally in your writing you wouldn't concern yourself any further with a case like this, as painful as it is for you when you think that this totally idealistic person is still in prison.

There is a formula that suggests that a particular sort of intellectual activity makes those who practice it into guardians or trustees of conscience; I find this formula empty, pompous, comical. Conscience cannot be delegated. I constantly witness this or that estimable intellectual stepping forward in the capacity of moral or political commentator, and I myself, when provoked by unpleasant current events, have not been able to avoid stepping forward in such a way. But immediately a reservation presents itself without which nothing works any more. Namely: anything you say to someone else, you should say exactly the same to yourself, at the very least. Avoid the appearance that you know better than the next person. Or even that you *are* better. Not an easy trick stylistically: to be critical, and yet to express in a credible way that you don't believe you know better than others. It would be even more difficult to put your two cents' worth into questions of conscience and still avoid the appearance that you are or think yourself better than those you criticize.

In every epoch there are themes or problems that are indisputably the themes of conscience for that epoch — or that have been made such. Two pieces of evidence for the themes of conscience of our epoch. A truly important thinker gave this formulation in 1992: "It is the reactions to right-wing terrorism — those from the political center in the general public, and those from above, from the government, the apparatus of state, and the party leadership — that make visible the full extent of our moral and political degradation." An equally important literary figure had stated a couple of years earlier: "Go into any restaurant in Salzburg. At first glance you have the impression that these are nothing but fine, upright people. But if you listen in to the conversations of your neighbors at the table, you discover that they dream only of genocide and gas chambers." If you add up what the thinker and the writer — both indeed equally serious — are saying, then the government, the apparatus of state, the party leadership, and the upright people at the next table are all "morally and politically" decadent. My first reaction, when year after year I read any number of such quotable statements from entirely serious eminences in the intellectual and literary realms, is: why doesn't it seem that way to me? What's wrong with my powers of perception? Or is it my too-easily-lulled conscience? For it's clear that these two eminences in the fields of intellect and language are also eminent in the field of conscience. Otherwise the sharpness with which they cast suspicion and even make accusations could not be explained. And if an accusation goes far enough, if it is convincing in and of itself, then proof becomes superfluous.

Finally a possibility arises to allow the speech to become critical. I hope that self-criticism may also be regarded as a kind of criticism. Why am I not mobilized by the outrage that commands the thinker to begin his sentence as follows: "When the sympathetic population sets up hot-dog stands in front of burning shelters for asylum-seekers . . ." You have to picture this: the population sympathizes with those who set fire to shelters for asylum-seekers, and thus they set up hot-dog stands in front of these burning shelters, to make some money on top of it. And I must admit that I would not be able to imagine this if I were not reading it in the leading intellectual weekly newspaper and under a name worthy of admiration. The weekly paper, a thousand miles distant from the tabloids, does one more thing to help along my insufficient powers of moral and political imagination: with the thinker's words it makes little boxes, printed in bold face for emphasis, so that you can take in the most important part even if you don't read the essay itself line by line. There the words of the thinker in extra big letters can be viewed thus: "Hot dog stands in front of burning shelters and symbolic politics for feeble minds." I cannot dispute such statements; the thinker as well as the writer are too eminent for me to do so. But — and this is obviously my moral and political shortcoming — no more can I agree with them. My reaction — entirely trivial, to be sure — to such painful statements: let's hope that what's being said to us in such blatant fashion isn't true. [And to reveal myself completely: I simply cannot believe these pain-inducing statements, which I can neither support nor refute.] It exceeds my moral and political imagination, so to speak, to regard what they say as true. Inside me an unprovable suspicion begins to take hold: those who come forward with such statements want to hurt us, because they think we deserve it. Probably they want to hurt themselves as well. But us too. All of us. With one restriction: all Germans. For this much is clear: in no other language in the last quarter of the twentieth century can one speak in such a way about an entire people, an entire population, an entire society. You can only say that about Germans. Or at most, as far as I can see, about Austrians as well.

Everyone knows the burden of our history, our everlasting disgrace. There is not a day in which it is not held up before us. Could it be that in doing so the intellectuals who hold it up before us fall prey for a moment to the illusion that, because they have labored once more in the grim service of memory, they have relieved their own guilt somewhat, that they are even for a moment closer to the victims than to the perpetrators? A momentary alleviation of the merciless confrontation of perpetrators and victims. I myself have never felt it possible to escape the side of the accused. Sometimes, when it seems I can't look anywhere without being attacked by an accusation, I must talk myself into believing, and thereby gaining some relief from the burden, that a routine of accusation has arisen in the media. Easily twenty times I have averted my eyes from the worst filmed sequences of concentration camps. No serious person denies Auschwitz; no person who is still of sound mind quibbles about the horror of Auschwitz; but when this past is held up to me every day in the media, I notice that something in me rebels against this unceasing presentation of our disgrace. Instead of being grateful for this never-ending presentation of our disgrace, I begin to look away. [I would like to understand why the past is being brought up in this decade more than ever before.] When I notice something in me rebelling, I try to seek out the motives of those holding up our disgrace, and I am almost happy when I believe I can discover that often the motive is no longer keeping alive the memory, or the impermissibility of forgetting, but rather the exploiting of our disgrace for present purposes. Always good and honorable purposes — but still exploitation. Someone disapproves of the way in which we propose to overcome the results of Germany's division, and says that in this way we are making a new Auschwitz possible. Even the division itself, as long as it lasted, was justified by leading intellectuals with a reference to Auschwitz. Another example: after exhaustive research, in one of my works I presented the story of a Jewish family and their journey from Landsberg an der Warthe to Berlin as an attempt, maintained over the course of fifty years, through baptism, marriage, and accomplishments to escape the lot of Eastern European Jews and become Germans, to assimilate completely. I said that anyone who sees everything as a road that could only end in Auschwitz makes the German-Jewish relationship into a catastrophe that was predestined under any and all circumstances. The intellectual who felt called on to comment called this a trivialization of Auschwitz. I will assume for my own sake that he could not possibly have studied the history of that family as thoroughly as I did. Even living members of that family have confirmed the accuracy of my depiction. But I'm still accused of trivializing Auschwitz. From there it's only a small step to denying the Holocaust. A clever intellectual on TV assumes a serious expression that on his face looks like a foreign language, when he shares with the world the author's serious failure, namely that Auschwitz does not appear in the book. Evidently he had never heard about the primal law of narration, that of narrative perspective. But even if he had, *Zeitgeist* comes before aesthetics.

Before one swallows all of this as a justified censure of one's lack of conscience, one would like to ask in return why, for example, in Goethe's novel *Wilhelm Meister,* which after all did not begin to appear until 1795, there is no mention of the guillotine. And when I see myself subjected to moral and political censure in this fashion, a memory forces its way into my consciousness. In 1977, not far from here in Bergen-Enkheim, I had to give a speech, and I used the occasion back then to make the following confession: "I find it unbearable to make German history end in a product of catastrophe, however bad its recent course has been." And: "We must grant as little recognition to West Germany, I say, trembling with my boldness, as we do to the East. We must keep open the wound called Germany." I think of this because once again now I tremble with my own audacity when I say: Auschwitz is not suited to become a routine threat, a means of intimidation or moral bludgeon that can be employed on any occasion, or even a compulsory exercise. All that comes into being through ritualization has the quality of lip service. But what suspicion does one invite when one says that the Germans today are a perfectly normal people, a perfectly ordinary society?

Posterity will be able to read one day, in all the discussions concerning the Holocaust Monument in Berlin, what people stirred up when they felt themselves responsible for the conscience of others: paving over the center of our capital to create a nightmare the size of a football field. The monumentalization of our disgrace. The historian Heinrich August Winkler calls this "negative nationalism." I dare to assert that this is not a bit better than its opposite, even if it appears a thousand times better. Probably there is a banality of the good too.[4]

Anything you say to someone else, you should say exactly the same to yourself, at the very least. It sounds like a cliché, but it's really nothing but wishful thinking. To speak of one's own failings in public? All of a sudden this too becomes just a phrase. The fact that such outcomes are difficult to avoid must have something to do with our conscience. When a thinker criticizes "the full extent of the moral and political degradation" of our government, apparatus of state, and party leaderships, then the impression cannot be avoided that he considers his conscience clearer than that of these morally and politically decadent souls. But what does that really feel like — a purer, a clearer, an immaculate conscience? To protect myself from further embarrassing confessions, I will call to my aid two intellectual giants whose understanding of language is beyond question: Heidegger and Hegel. Heidegger in his 1927 work *Being and Time:* "Becoming certain of not having done something does not possess the character of a phenomenon of conscience. On the contrary: this becoming certain of not having done something can sooner mean a forgetting of conscience." That is, put less precisely: a clear conscience is as perceptible as the lack of a headache. But then it is said in the paragraph of *Being and Time* about conscience: "Being guilty is part of being itself." I hope that this won't once again be understood right away as a convenient phrase for letting off the hook those contemporary obscurantists who don't want to feel guilty. And now Hegel. Hegel writes in his *Philosophy of Right:* "Conscience, that deepest inward solitude within oneself, where all that is external and all that is limited disappears, this thoroughgoing withdrawal into one's self."

---

[4] A reference to Hannah Arendt's famous phrase "the banality of evil" in her *Eichmann in Jerusalem.*

The result of this philosophical assistance: A clear conscience is no conscience at all. Everyone is alone with his or her conscience. For this reason, public acts of conscience are in danger of becoming symbolic. And nothing is more alien to conscience than symbolism, however well-intentioned. This "thoroughgoing withdrawal into one's self" cannot be represented. It must remain "inward solitude." You can't demand from others what you would like to receive but are not willing to give — or cannot give. And this is not just German idealist philosophy. It is, for example, put into practice in literature — in Kleist's play *The Prince of Homburg*. And now I can share something beautiful after all. Wonderful scenes in Kleist's play in which the conscience is respected, perhaps even celebrated, as the epitome of the personal. The cavalry general Prince of Homburg has acted contrary to orders in battle; the Elector condemns him to death and then suddenly announces: "He is pardoned!" Natalie can scarcely believe it: "He is pardoned? He's not going to die now?" she asks. The Elector replies: "I bear deep within me, as is well known to you, the highest respect for his moral feeling; if he can regard the sentence as unjust, I will quash the sentence: he goes free!" Thus it is made entirely dependent on the moral feeling of the condemned man whether the sentence of death is carried out. If the condemned man can regard the sentence as unjust, he is free.

This is the freedom of conscience I'm talking about. Conscience, left to itself, creates enough illusion. But when it is commanded publicly, only illusion rules. Does not each person nurture and conceal deep within himself a cabinet of mirrors designed for the production of self-esteem? Is not each person an institution for the licensing of the most irreconcilable contradictions? Is not each person a conveyor belt for an endless dialectic of truth and lies? Each person a warrior of conscience led by vanity? Or am I generalizing too much here, just to find company for my own weakness? I cannot omit the question: would the general public really be poorer or coarser in conscience if poets and thinkers had not come forward as guardians of the national conscience? Examples, please. In my favorite decade, 1790 to 1800, Schiller, Fichte, Hegel, Hölderlin are supporters of the French Revolution. Goethe, who has been a state official in Weimar since 1776 and raised to the nobility since 1782, makes a wartime journey in the anti-revolutionary camp with his royal patron the Duke of Weimar; before Verdun, it is said, he observes prismatic colors on small fish in an earthenware crater. One month after the outbreak of the revolution he has completed his most tender and intimate autobiographical drama, *Tasso*. And when he meets Schiller in 1794 at the "Society of Scientific Researchers," their friendship, it is said, is definitively established. And apparently it did not disturb either of them that the other cultivated a different sort of conscience than himself. Which one of them was the conscience of his century? Is it now because of the greatness of these two men that a friendship arose between two truly different consciences? Or was there still tolerance back then? Tolerance — a foreign word[5] that, because of the fact that what it designates no longer occurs, is today rather dispensable. Another example concerning conscience: Thomas Mann. Shortly before 1918 he rejects democracy, and writes that it is "alien to our land, something translated from abroad that can never turn into German life and German truth. . . . Politics . . ., democracy is in and of itself something un-German, anti-German. . . ." And in 1922, in honor of Gerhart Hauptmann's sixtieth birthday, he gives a speech "On the German Republic" in which he says: ". . . just to prove that democracy, that a republic can attain an advanced level of culture, even the level of German Romanticism: this is why I have stepped onto this podium." And he remained on that podium. But for twenty years prior to that he had been an intellectual and an author, however — as far as public opinion is concerned — on the other side politically. But someone reading his books from *Buddenbrooks* to *The Magic Mountain* learns practically nothing of this dramatic change in his opinion. To make up for it, though, this reader gets the real Thomas Mann. The way he really thought and felt — in short, his morality — is conveyed to the reader in Mann's novels and stories spontaneously and more reliably than in the texts where he felt compelled to be correct in a political and moral sense. Or even had the feeling that he needed to justify himself.

One would like to confront the soldiers of public opinion with this example when they, with moral pistol extended, force the writer into the service of opinion. In any event, they have brought matters to the point where writers no longer need to be read, only interviewed. The fact that the pronouncements that arise in this way are either not verifiable or flatly contradicted in the works of those authors is a matter of no concern to the guardians of opinion and conscience, since the literary text has no utility for them.

[I admit, the author has only himself to blame if he engages in this borrowed language and, because of a simple need of legitimation, acts as if he could comment on this and that and the other issue. And the more famous a writer becomes, the more he's considered responsible for this

---

[5] The word "Toleranz," though widely used in German, has Latin rather than Germanic roots.

and that and the other. But he's responsible only for himself, and then only if he doesn't let himself be talked out of it. And it's only because he's responsible only for himself that he can be useful to others as well, precisely because what is important is important only because we all have it in common. But this usefulness cannot be striven for and cannot be served up; it is produced only in the most beautifully innocent collaboration in the world, namely that between the author and the reader. This arises through a single condition: the reasons that bring us to write and to read are the same. The need to spell out our existence. Whether it is in reading or in writing is of secondary importance. This relationship, which is of crucial importance for the writer, needs no such half-baked wishful statements as: anything you say to someone else, you should say exactly the same to yourself. In the context of involuntary reading and writing, this is more than a little bit problematic. The novel and the poem are never addressed first to someone else. They are addressed to that someone else only when they awaken the interest of that person; then the interested person becomes active and produces meaning, where an uninterested person sees only jungles of letters. Stay with your difficulties. They are the difficulties of living. They are awakened not by the pulpits of speakers but by breathing in and out. The needs that emerge in the course of living become language, a language that cannot be commanded.] Does there exist any language outside of literature that does not have the intention of selling me something? I know of none. That's why nothing makes one so free as the language of literature (see Kleist).

My trust in language has developed through the experience that it helps me when I don't believe I already know something. It holds back, doesn't even awaken, so to speak, when I think I know something already that I just need to formulate with the help of language. An undertaking like that has no appeal for it. It calls me self-righteous then. And it will not awaken just to help me to be right. For instance, when I have to give a critical speech, because it's Sunday morning and the world is bad, and this society is of course particularly bad, and anyway everything is dull without a few insults thrown in; when I sense that it would violate my inner feeling to accommodate myself once again to this ersatz-preacher function, then I give myself up to language, I put the reins in its hand, not caring where it leads me. That last statement of course isn't quite right. I seize the reins whenever I fear that it will go too far, betray too much of me, reveal too much of my unpresentability. Then, fearfully and cautiously, I mobilize linguistic concealment routines of every kind. The goal of such a Sunday speech would then appear to me at best that the listeners at the end of my speech don't think they know me as well as they did at the beginning. The speaker who puts his trust in language may aspire to achieve the result that the listener does not know the speaker at the end of the speech as well as he or she did before. But the speaker cannot suppress a very daring hope[, as a kind of apotheosized dodge]: namely, that inasmuch as he is not "known" as clearly and distinctly as he was before the speech, he has by the same token become more familiar to his listeners. [That is a bit overblown, even when said in the homestretch.] It should simply be permitted to hope that one might serve others not only by increasing their knowledge, but also, as one language person speaking to another, by brushing against their being in a way that cannot be calculated, but that perhaps can be experienced. That is purely a hope. [But I do want to conclude with one suspicion. The first word in the just-published book of a young author is "suspicion." Then she continues: "I suspect that everything is much more beautiful than people acknowledge. Everything is much more beautiful than people have been able to express up to now. And people have been able to say quite a lot up to now, for we have already accomplished quite a lot in an attempt to express how beautiful things are. We make new attempts and we always try to find new ways to express how beautiful everything is. But still, things are more beautiful than people can say."

That's it on the topic of the beautiful. The author I quoted is Johanna Walser.[6]] Now all I have left to say is: honored Mr. President, please let Mr. Rainer Rupp go.[7] For dear peace's sake.

---

[6] The author's daughter.

[7] The imprisoned East German spy referred to earlier in the speech.

Commentary

WALSER'S INITIAL FOCUS is on the opposition between private speech, specifically literary speech, and public utterance. The title — "Experiences While Composing a Sunday Speech" — seems to point solely at the private sphere, suggesting that what we are about to hear is not the speech itself but a record of the speaker's thoughts and experiences while writing the speech. In keeping with his admonition in "Handshake with Ghosts," he begins in the third person, speaking of getting the news about winning the *Peace Prize of the German Book Trade* and referring to himself as "the prizewinner." But then two sentences later he shifts to the second person: "You've given this speech before. So give it again, for God's sake." The second paragraph then begins with a return to the third person ("the prizewinner" again), then another foray into the second person, then a return to the third person. But then, in the middle of the second paragraph, he makes an abrupt transition from third person to first:

> But then, when he was told explicitly that he was expected to give a critical sermon, his freedom-loving soul rebelled once more. It was clear to me too that I would have to justify my potpourri of the beautiful.

And from this point on, there is hardly a paragraph without any first-person forms. This at-first-inexplicable shifting of narrative perspective can usefully be related to the antithesis developed by Volker Nölle in a recent article,[8] namely: is this a literary artist who is temporarily assuming the role of public speaker (in which case the first person would be expected), or is this a public speaker who is assuming the role of literary artist, thus playing with literary conventions such as third-person narrative? As Nölle points out, this is the most significant of the ambiguities that are present in the text.

A related question is the dilemma posed from the start: on the one hand, the speaker's desire to speak about something beautiful, whether artistic or natural beauty, and on the other hand, his awareness of the public expectation that he deliver a critical sermon, a "Sunday speech," devoted to some theme in current political or social affairs. À propos of this dilemma, he makes the first of several references to unnamed authors or intellectuals: "It's no longer a crime to talk about trees, because in the

[8] Volker Nölle, "Der Redner als Dichter und umgekehrt: Zu konzeptionellen Aporien in Walsers Friedenspreisrede," in *Seelenarbeit an Deutschland: Martin Walser in Perspective,* ed. Stuart Parkes and Fritz Wefelmeyer (Amsterdam: Rodopi, 2004), 259–80.

meantime so many of them have gotten sick." Unlike the others, this reference to the famous line from Brecht's "To Those Born After" would be familiar to his German audience. The tone is clearly sarcastic, implying a rejection of Brecht's statement that to speak of beautiful things in a time of crisis shows a criminal indifference to the sufferings of others. This is closely related to the theme he returns to at various points of the speech, namely his questioning of the premise, generally shared by German writers who resisted the Nazi regime and since that time, that writers must be public spokesmen, that they should in effect be the conscience of the nation. As in the passage discussed earlier from "Handshake with Ghosts," he argues that such public statements do not contain or express one's genuine self. Later in the speech he gives the example of Thomas Mann, pointing to his political about-face, from scorning democracy as "un-German" during the First World War to defending the Weimar Republic; anyone reading Mann's literary works during these years, Walser claims, would not see any such shift, and it is in these literary texts that Mann's true self is revealed.

Taken in a vacuum, this criticism might seem valid. There is no doubt — and the examples of Brecht and Mann, as different as they were in their politics and otherwise, serve to underline the point — that German writers since the 1930s or even earlier have felt compelled to take a stand on public issues in a way that is not expected of writers in the United States or elsewhere. Thus one might well question whether this compulsion, however appropriate it may have been in the 1930s and 1940s, is still needed today. But then the question arises as to whether Walser's speech is consistent with this premise; that is, is it truly the speaker as literary artist, and not in fact the literary artist as speaker?

Returning to the question of whether to speak about something beautiful or give a critical sermon, Walser speaks of his own desire to avoid dealing with unpleasant matters: "I close my eyes to evils to whose elimination I cannot contribute." In this context he first uses the terms "thinking about something else" and "looking away," which later in the speech are explicitly related to images of the Holocaust; the motif of "looking away" clearly recalls the last paragraph of "No End to Auschwitz." However, whereas in his 1979 speech he speaks of the necessity of forcing himself to look in spite of the urge to look away, here he seems to regard "looking away" as a desirable gift that he has struggled to learn. From the defense of "looking away" he proceeds immediately to another issue, the relevance of which is not immediately apparent, namely the question of whether everything must be atoned for: "I am also of the opinion that not everything must be atoned for. I couldn't live in a world in which everything had to be atoned for." The notion of atonement is then applied to the case of the East German spy Rainer Rupp (who is not named until the last line of the speech) who was imprisoned in spite of the finding that he was motivated in part by the desire to promote peace by making the intentions of NATO forces transparent to the Soviet bloc.

This rather unmotivated shift of focus — from the notion of "looking away" to a questioning of the necessity of atonement, and from there to a principled stance against the unfair punishment of someone who was motivated only by idealism — deserves some examination, especially since he returns to the case of the East German spy in the last line of his speech, this time actually naming him. By pleading for mercy in this case, as the speechmaker explicitly states, he is complying with the expectation that he give a "Sunday speech." And this particular cause, it must be said, is calculated not to raise hackles among the left-wing intellectuals who predictably would and did take offense at other portions of the speech. Further, as Volker Nölle points out, he undercuts this plea by admitting that he would not have made it were it not for the pressure to say something critical, and that it won't accomplish anything (he speaks of "foreseeable ineffectuality"). Finally, by appearing magnanimous in pleading that atonement is not necessary for Rupp's "crime," he is preparing the ground for his argument that the same holds true for crimes of a greater order of magnitude — that is, for Auschwitz.

From there his free associations take him to the related issue of conscience, at which time he makes the statement "Conscience cannot be delegated," thus opening up another of the main themes of the speech: the notion that conscience is a private matter and that for any public intellectual to pose as a public conscience or moral authority is "empty, pompous, comical" — though he is forced to admit that he has adopted this role on occasion. But he adds a necessary condition: anything you tell others you must tell yourself as well. He then proceeds to discuss the "topics of conscience of our epoch," quoting various unnamed public intellectuals who speak of the "moral and political degradation" and xenophobia of the German and Austrian public. Rather than refuting any of these intellectuals, or even naming them, he offers this response:

> I cannot dispute such statements; the thinker as well as the writer are too eminent for me to do so. But — and this is obviously my moral and political shortcoming — no more can I agree with them. My reaction — entirely trivial, to be sure — to such painful statements: let's hope that what's being said to us in such blatant fashion isn't true. It exceeds my moral-political imagination, so to speak, to regard what they say as true.

Here again it must be pointed out that the "fictional" frame of the speech — that is, a stream-of-consciousness narrative of the thought process of someone writing a speech — relieves the author of any obligation to engage the writers he is quoting, or even of naming them; instead they are referred to, with obvious sarcasm, in such phrases as "a truly important thinker," "an equally important literary figure," "eminences in the intellectual and literary realms." And then he proceeds to make a crucial claim:

> . . . those who come forward with such statements want to hurt us, because they think we deserve it. Probably they want to hurt themselves as well. But us too. All of us. With one restriction: all Germans.

These criticisms are thus motivated by a malicious intent: the desire to hurt Germans.

It is at this point that he proceeds to the most notorious portion of the speech. He begins thus:

> Everyone knows the burden of our history, our everlasting shame. There is not a day in which it is not held up before us. Could it be that in doing so the intellectuals who hold it up before us fall prey for a moment to the illusion that, because they have labored once more in the grim service of memory, they have relieved their own guilt somewhat, that they are even for a moment closer to the victims than to the perpetrators? A momentary alleviation of the merciless confrontation of perpetrators and victims. I myself have never felt it possible to escape the side of the accused.

His wording is revealing in many respects. First, where in his earlier texts he spoke of Germans' collective responsibility for the Holocaust, here he speaks only of a "burden" (thus presenting Germans as victims) and a "shame" (thus downgrading guilt into a kind of public disgrace). He conjectures that those intellectuals who constantly beat the drum of German guilt, past and present, fall prey to the illusion that they can thereby identify with the victims rather than the perpetrators, and then he states, with apparent pride, that he has never thought it possible to leave the side of the "accused." This is reminiscent of the passage in "Our Auschwitz" that similarly postulates an unbridgeable gulf between the victims and survivors and their families on the one hand, and the perpetrators and their descendents on the other. But what in the earlier essay seemed a stance of exemplary moral courage takes on a more problematic aspect thirty years later: the category of "us Germans" that he invokes is seemingly constituted by the burden of past guilt and thus by implication excludes those who are not descended from Germans of the Nazi era, notably Jews and other minorities in Germany. At the same time the term "accused" suggests that their guilt has not been proved, and in invoking the notion of a defendant in a criminal trial he again opens up the notion of Germans as victims. And at this point he explicitly connects the notion of "looking away" with the Holocaust ("Easily twenty times I have averted my eyes from the worst filmed sequences of concentration camps") and continues:

> No serious person denies Auschwitz; no person who is still of sound mind quibbles about the horror of Auschwitz; but when this past is held up to me every day in the media, I notice that something in me rebels against this unceasing presentation of our disgrace.

From here he proceeds to the accusation that the intellectuals responsible for this "unceasing presentation" intend the "exploitation of our disgrace for present purposes." He refers to some of the criticism he had drawn in recent years, for example his omission of any Holocaust reference in his autobiographical novel *A Springing Fountain,* and the related accusation of a "trivialization of Auschwitz," and summarizes the apparent obliviousness to basic principles of narrative with the sarcastic comment "*Zeitgeist* comes before aesthetics." This is, he suggests, as if someone were to criticize Goethe's *Wilhelm Meister* for failing to mention the guillotine. Here he once again cites his Bergen-Enkheim speech of 1977: "We must keep open the wound called Germany." What, one might well ask at this juncture, is the connection of this to his previous point? Only his feeling of being "subjected to moral and political censure." This feeling enables him to make a leap from his trepidation on the former occasion to the same feelings at present, and then to launch into the most notorious passage in the speech:

> I think of this because once again now I tremble with my own audacity when I say: Auschwitz is not suited to become a routine threat, a means of intimidation or moral bludgeon that can be employed on any occasion, or even a compulsory exercise. All that comes into being through ritualization has the quality of lip service. But what suspicion does one invite when one says that the Germans today are a perfectly normal people, a perfectly ordinary society?

Auschwitz as a "moral bludgeon": the phrase has become famous in Germany in the years since the speech was given. What has generally escaped notice is that his protest against the alleged use of Auschwitz as a bludgeon to keep Germans in a condition of shame is followed immediately by what he frames as the most daring claim of all: that the Germans are a normal people, an ordinary society. In contrast to the truly provocative comments about the exploitation of the Holocaust, and the similarly notorious comments that follow, in which he calls the planned Holocaust Monument in Berlin "a nightmare the size of a football field," few if any have regarded this plea for Germany's normalcy as controversial.

Having committed his "taboo violation" in the discussion of the Holocaust, the speaker then returns to a more defensive mode, quoting Heidegger and Hegel on conscience and summarizing: "A clear conscience is no conscience at all. Everyone is alone with his or her conscience. For this reason, public acts of conscience are in danger of becoming symbolic."[9] He speaks of "freedom of conscience," quotes from Heinrich von Kleist's *Prince of Homburg,* and refers to the fact that Goethe and Schiller formed a friendship in the 1790s even though they had taken very different stances vis-à-vis the French Revolution —⟶ something that he attributes also to "tolerance," which (he claims) is no longer to be found nowadays. Then follows his excursus on Thomas Mann, referred to earlier, in which he suggests that Mann's public pronouncements had little to do with the *real* Mann, who is revealed in his literary works.

This leads him to the last substantive section of the speech, in which he speaks with some eloquence of the uniqueness of literary language, and his hope to connect with his audience on a plane that does not correspond to that of the everyday political discourse that otherwise dominates:

> The speaker who puts his trust in language may aspire to achieve the result that the listener does not know the speaker at the end of the speech as well as he or she did before. But the speaker cannot suppress a very daring hope . . .: namely, that inasmuch as he is not "known" as clearly and distinctly as he was before the speech, he has by the same token become more familiar to his listeners. [. . .] It should simply be permitted to hope that one might serve others not only by increasing their knowledge, but also, as one language person speaking to another, by brushing against their being in a way which cannot be calculated, but which perhaps can be experienced.

To return to the categories suggested by Volker Nölle, it seems that here he definitively chooses the role of "public speaker as literary artist" once and for all, refusing the role of a writer as public spokesman delivering a "Sunday speech" in favor of the speaker who is calling his audience's attention to the "other world" of literary language.

But then, as if to defeat any possibility of a final resolution of the dilemma, he returns to the opposite role, and pleads in the final sentence

[9] Nölle, "Der Redner als Dichter und umgekehrt," 37.

for the release of the East German spy. And to eliminate any doubt that he is now a "literary artist as public speaker" in the realm of politics, he calls the spy by name, thus eliminating any fictional or hypothetical dimension to his plea. And he makes the plea "in the name of dear peace," thus paying homage to the name of his prize.

*   *   *

Given the bitter controversy that arose in the wake of this speech — with Ignatz Bubis and others accusing Walser of deliberately inciting right-wing and antisemitic sentiment, and Walser's defenders asserting that he had done nothing but offer an entirely appropriate, and much-needed, critique of Germany's culture of remembrance — the question of course arises as to how to view the speech now, ten years after its delivery.

To begin with the most serious charge, that he had intentionally given encouragement and license to those with right-wing leanings, it should be pointed out that when, after two months of angry exchanges, the two men actually met together (in the offices of the *FAZ*), Bubis did withdraw the charge that Walser had intended to feed far-right sentiment. The fact that these voices cited Walser in support of their views cannot be denied, though. The question then becomes: can or should Walser be held responsible for these voices on the fringe of German public opinion? In response to this, a case can certainly be made that given Germany's past, responsible German citizens should exercise particular care not to validate the sentiments of neo-Nazi or similar groups. On the other hand, it can also be argued that because of Germany's past, the significance of these groups is greatly exaggerated in the international media; though this is perhaps less true now than in the first postwar decades, it remains true that an act of antisemitic or xenophobic violence or desecration in Germany will receive more attention in the press than a similar act committed in other European countries. Given this, one can understand Walser's impatience with those both inside and outside Germany who take these fringe groups as representative of all Germans. A balanced response might be on the one hand to assert that Germans do bear a special responsibility to keep watch and give no encouragement to xenophobic voices, but at the same time to reject the notion that these voices are typical of Germans as a whole.

As to the specific charge that the Holocaust is being exploited for various purposes, this is a complex issue. Walser's charge, on the face of it, is not that different from the argument made by the American Jewish historian Peter Novick in his controversial book *The Holocaust in Amer-*

ican Life,[10] and considerably less extreme than Norman Finkelstein's provocative book *The Holocaust Industry*.[11] It is certainly an arguable proposition that the memory of the Holocaust is invoked by Jewish and other groups in support of various causes; this does not imply an ignoble or immoral activity, but it is at least one that might give pause for reflection. What is most problematic in Walser's presentation is that, given the "personal" and "literary" mode he adopts for much of the speech, he is able to avoid naming specific individuals or groups who are engaged in this "exploitation." The specific passages he quotes in the speech have been identified as coming from left-wing German or Austrian intellectuals or writers, so in a narrow sense Walser can be defended against the charge made by Bubis and others that Walser was taking aim at the efforts around 1999 by Holocaust survivors and the families of victims to obtain reparations. But the lack of specificity in his indictment, and in particular his formulation "they want to hurt us" can certainly evoke the sense that these are outsiders who want to hurt Germans, and Jewish groups and individuals seeking reparations would thus be a likely association.

Quite apart from the question of who is doing the "exploiting," there is the larger issue of Germany's culture of remembrance, with the Berlin Holocaust Monument as its most tangible symbol. It must be remembered that in the 1960s, when Walser wrote "Our Auschwitz," there was little discussion of the Holocaust in the German public sphere, and it was virtually ignored in school curricula. As pointed out earlier, though, the situation was to change dramatically in the late 1970s and since. Walser's was and is certainly not the only voice suggesting that there is a danger of overdoing it, that Germans of all generations will tend to "look away" when they feel overly bombarded with images and reminders of the Holocaust. And yet Walser's emphasis on conscience as a purely individual matter, and his simultaneous shift from the notion of collective guilt to collective shame or disgrace, are problematic. In an answer to his critics that was printed in the *FAZ* one month after his speech, Walser wrote: "To what does shame bear witness, if not to crimes?"[12] But this is hardly persuasive. The word "Schande" in German, like its English equivalents "shame" or "disgrace," suggests a feeling that can be evoked by many things other than crimes, including embarrass-

---

[10] Peter Novick, *The Holocaust in American Life* (Boston: Houghton-Mifflin, 1999).

[11] Norman Finkelstein, *The Holocaust Industry: Reflections on the Exploitation of Jewish Suffering* (London and New York: Verso, 2000).

[12] *Die Walser-Bubis Debatte: Eine Dokumentation*, ed. Frank Schirrmacher (Frankfurt am Main: Suhrkamp, 1999), 252–60.

ment at wearing inappropriate dress or similar social faux pas. And as to
the question of individual versus collective conscience, we might recall
Walser's own words in his 1979 essay "Handshake with Ghosts": "A
liberal society that shuns the religious and everything that transcends the
individual self. . . can only repress Auschwitz. Where the ego is supreme,
one can only repress guilt. One can absorb, retain, and bear it only
together with others." Whereas in 1979 he seemed to insist on a collective effort to deal with Germany's past, in his 1998 speech he seems to
advocate precisely the kind of withdrawal into the private sphere that he
had condemned earlier. Finally, as to the Berlin Holocaust Monument
(which, it must be remembered, was still in the planning stage when
Walser spoke), responses to the location, size, and design of the monument have been many and varied, and there are legitimate issues to be
raised about all three. But to reject it as a "nightmare the size of a
football field" is clearly not a helpful contribution to this ongoing discussion. Once again, the fictional stance suggested in the speech's title,
and its occasional use of third-person forms to indicate the speaker,
relieve him from any necessity of engaging in a substantive critique,
allowing him to express a merely personal aversion — but one which,
given the public setting of the speech, clearly encourages his audience to
give voice to similar sentiments. In the ensuing debate, Walser's frequent
references to the thousands of letters he had received in support of his
position certainly point to his concern with expressing not only a personal view but also one he believed was shared by many if not most of his
fellow Germans.

Finally, the one aspect that was troubling even in his 1965 essay —
the gap he posits between victims and perpetrators, which also separates
their descendents several generations later — remains troubling. As he
had earlier, he dismisses as an "illusion" the notion that by working in
the "grim service of memory" one can alleviate, if only for the moment,
the "merciless confrontation of perpetrators and victims." It is interesting
to note that in the course of their face-to-face conversation in December
1998, Walser and Bubis did seem to reach agreement on one point.
Walser stated that "there are observances centered on the victims and
others centered on the perpetrators, and there is little in common between them. . . . We have not yet found the mode of remembrance," to
which Bubis replied: "We must find a path for mutual remembrance."[13]
Skeptics on both sides of the divide might suggest that this goal is
unrealistic, that the memories of victims and their descendents can never

[13] Schirrmacher, *Walser-Bubis Debatte,* 461.

be brought into accord with those of perpetrators and their descendents. And yet, increasingly with the passing of time and the emergence of new generations, this seems a goal worth pursuing, even if it can never wholly be achieved.

On Talking to Yourself:
A Flagrant Attempt (2000)

Context

THE WALSER-BUBIS DEBATE, OCCASIONED BY Walser's Peace Prize speech and Bubis's ensuing accusation that Walser had made inflammatory remarks, is widely considered the most prominent debate regarding the German past and how it should be viewed by Germans today since the Historian's Debate of the mid-1980s. Though at first it seemed that Bubis was alone in his criticism of Walser's speech, his voice would soon be joined by many others who were similarly disturbed by the speech. The media reflected this turn as well, going from what was for the most part an uncritical celebration of Walser to what was at times a total demonization of him for alleged right-wing or antisemitic views. Though Walser, in this speech and elsewhere, had questioned the role of the public sphere, he clearly attached great importance to the support he received from many people (in his conversation with Bubis he made several references to the thousands of letters he had received in support of his stance), and he was likewise deeply wounded by the criticisms he received, and he expressed his anger, notably in a lecture at the University of Duisburg, at what he felt was a total misunderstanding of what he had said.

When he and Bubis had their face-to-face meeting in the offices of the *FAZ* two months after the speech, Walser seemed oblivious to Bubis's attempts at conciliation and at one point displayed what even his sympathetic biographer Jörg Magenau refers to as "unbelievable tactlessness": speaking of his decades-long attempt to deal with the Holocaust and its meaning for Germany, he said to Bubis "I was involved with this subject while you were still dealing with entirely different matters." Bubis was a Holocaust survivor whose father had been murdered in Treblinka, but Walser was referring to his activities as a Frankfurt real-estate specu-

lator in the 1960s, which had formed the basis for the German film director Rainer Werner Fassbinder's controversial play *Der Müll, die Stadt
und der Tod* (*Garbage, the City, and Death*). Thus his instinctive disdain
for Bubis's early business ventures, fostered by his originally left-wing
political orientation, blinded him to the fact that Bubis had "dealt with"
the Holocaust far earlier, and much more directly, than he himself had.
Though, as mentioned earlier, there was a moment of near-agreement
toward the end of the conversation, in which both men acknowledged
the need to find a mode of common remembrance of the past, the meeting can hardly be regarded as a success. Bubis, who had devoted much of
his later life to promoting the possibility of a renewed Jewish community
in Germany, was devastated by the entire experience, and in an interview
shortly thereafter expressed his feeling that his life's work had been in
vain and asked to be buried in Israel.

Walser, who had for some time been critical of the role of the media
in creating public opinion, felt he was being victimized and withdrew increasingly into the private sphere. He became embroiled in bitter exchanges even with Siegfried Unseld, the editor of Suhrkamp Press, which
had published his works for almost fifty years.

The year 1999 was also marked by the NATO bombing campaign
directed against the Serbian Yugoslav leadership in defense of the ethnic
Albanians in Kosovo. This was a watershed in postwar German history,
as it marked the first time since the Second World War that the German military had participated in an armed conflict. Germany's left-wing
foreign minister Joschka Fischer supported this NATO action, but it
was opposed by many intellectuals. Walser makes reference to this in
the following essay. This essay, written in 1999 and published the following year, takes as its main issue the tension between public and
private utterance.

Martin Walser: On Talking to Yourself:
A Flagrant Attempt (2000)

1.

THE THOUGHTS THAT GO THROUGH YOUR MIND on their own are different from those that you can summon up. If you force yourself to think about something, or if some external force causes or forces you to think about something, then this thinking takes place mainly in the same language in which the thing you're supposed to think about is dealt with on the outside. The sentences that pass through my head involuntarily are at home in a language completely different from that of the sentences that are offered to or forced on me from the outside. I believe that writers, when they're writing, are completely subject to and under the spell of this language that arises in them involuntarily. It is their language. They don't control it, but if they're lucky, it controls them.

Once, when I gave a speech in Munich denouncing German complicity in the American War in Vietnam, a woman in the audience said in the discussion: "Mr. Walser, you're always so progressive in your speeches, but in your novels you're not like that at all." I replied that the novels probably convey who I am more precisely than do the speeches. Since that time, a kind of mistrust of public opinions has grown up inside me. That doesn't mean that I could have gotten by without opinions when writing essays or speeches, or that I could get by without them now. It also doesn't mean that I would want to criticize others — journalists, politicians, or professors, for instance — if they express themselves primarily in opinions and prefer to set themselves apart from others through their opinions. It means simply that as a writer I have had the experience that there's less of me in my opinions than in my novels. Of course characters in novels can't get by without having opinions. But the sum of all the opinions of all the characters in a novel still doesn't amount to the opinion of the author. A novel simply isn't allowed to amount to an opinion. Every author of a novel knows this, without necessarily having to know that he knows it. Even a drama isn't allowed to amount to an opinion. And — I'd like to express this wish today — neither should

---

Walser uses the term "Selbstgespräch," which can be translated as "soliloquy," but since that term in English is associated mainly with the theater, I've chosen to translate it variously as "talking with or to yourself," "internal conversation," and so on.

a speech and an essay. I don't have anything to advocate. I don't need to educate or enlighten anyone except myself.[1] Enlightenment and enlightened: these are two words that serve to characterize intellectual languages as the correct languages. The intellectual who knows beyond a doubt that his writing is enlightened proves this most often by accusing another intellectual of being unenlightened. May it not surprise one that enlightenment today always seems to be directed at others? This is how it's become established: to see yourself in the service of enlightenment means to tell others what they should know or what they should take to heart. Originally, enlightenment did not amount to reproaching others for being insufficiently enlightened. Kant's famous sentence on enlightenment, after all, reads as follows: "Enlightenment is man's emergence from his self-created immaturity." And: "For this enlightenment nothing is needed except freedom." What I see in these words is more an exploration of the self than an instructing of others. That's why I'm surprised that people divorce these venerable words from their function, in which they expressed the potential for liberation, and use them instead as a seal of approval for their own manner of expression. Kant calls it a goal of enlightenment that people should be capable of "using their own understanding securely and well in matters of religion without the guidance of another." And a prince may be considered enlightened, says Kant, if he allows each person "to make use of his own reason in everything that is a matter of conscience." In the meantime, left-wing intellectuals have taken out a lease on the Enlightenment for their particular concerns of the current moment. All else is declared anti-Enlightenment. In 1972 I used this formulation: "The basic contradiction between labor and capital is as unresolved now as it was formerly." Without having said it explicitly back then, I doubtless felt myself to be serving the cause of enlightenment. Today I could no longer say that sentence. It wouldn't convey who I am any more. I believe that, even back then, sentences like that didn't really convey who I was. Today I hope that opposing labor and capital to one another in that way was too abstract from the start. Perhaps it still made more sense in the nineteenth century than it does in the second half of the twentieth. And everything that I can come up with on this topic entitles me only to make maybe-sentences, not to any general suspicion of capitalism. Today I'd have to demand of myself that I put any such statement I make into active practice. I could express a

[1] In these sentences Walser uses the German noun *Aufklärung* and the associated verb *aufklären*. The noun designates the historical period of the Enlightenment and the progressive values associated with it, but it can also refer to the process of enlightening or educating, as does the verb.

general suspicion of the executive offices of capitalism, if only I knew how to make that suspicion into a certainty and then how to turn that certainty into a more favorable, more public-minded economic reality. To look good to myself merely by stating an opinion wouldn't be enough for me today. I still know why I made these anticapitalist formulations back then. I saw myself—because of my guilty conscience—as a "laborer in the production of public opinion." This claim, or this way of currying favor, was mediated by the experience of dependence. I might still be able to say that the intellectual is not a "free" writer, or as the case may be, that the freelance writer is dependent—on the market, on the publishing house, on public opinion. In 1972 I said that because we are dependent entities, "we have the obligation constantly to pronounce the shortcomings in our democracy." "These shortcomings are still great and fundamental," I said. "We won't solve the problem pragmatically with one or two small cosmetic operations." That's what I said. "Socialism and democracy are two words" for an "imaginable condition in our homeland."[2] That's what I said. And I spoke out against "the myths of immobility" and the "zeal of desperation" and in favor of "our ability to shape human history." You could relate everything that one person, or that many people then were saying, to one single word: justice. More justice. In the workplace. And the most important factor in producing injustice in the workplace, in my experience, was and still is dependence. Dependence distorts reality.

When, without intending to do so, I witness how I write a novel that tells of the distortion that takes place due to dependence, I notice that this involuntary writing expresses more of what's inside me than when I mobilize opinions inside me that oppose capitalism as the source of this distorting dependence. And I can hope, though it could never be proved, that this writing, which expresses more of me, communicates more to others than any opinion I could possibly utter.

That woman in Munich was probably right: I'm progressive in my speeches but not in my novels. The novel arises involuntarily. It announces itself as an increasing necessity to respond to an experience. Usually a painful experience. A lack of something. But this lack was never the unresolved basic contradiction between capital and labor but rather a lack of existence. This lack too has societal causes; but when you respond to this in a novel, and in doing so entrust yourself to language, then this

[2] Walser uses the word "Heimat," which had caused a stir in 1980 when he published a collection of essays entitled *Heimatlob* (Praise of Homeland), since it was a rather taboo term because of its associations with extreme nationalist movements and with the Nazi past. By 2000, though, the word no longer elicited such reactions.

means you believe that whatever your experiences have brought about inside you will come out if you don't want to do anything else but write. Write a novel, for instance. This means: you don't express yourself directly, but rather in your characters. The novel becomes socially meaningful only through its reader. About whom you don't have to — in fact you can't — think while writing. The reader can respond to a book only if he has had experiences that the author has had as well, and to which the author has responded by writing the book. Thus consciousness can arise. Perhaps even meaning. But it's just that this meaning cannot be produced intentionally, it can only arise on its own: within the reader, through the reader. It is perhaps more a product of the reader than of the author.

The unabridged quotation that says that books have their own destinies reads as follows: Procaptu lectoris habent sua fata libelli. The scholar Manfred Fuhrmann translates it as follows: "Books have a destiny that depends on the capacity of the reader." Ancient lyric poetry was seen — I know this too from Manfred Fuhrmann, who quotes Richard Heinze — as "addressing a person who was imagined to be present." All that's left of this for us, or at least for me, is language. The element of potential commonality. But also an element for divisions. Internal languages, external languages, adopted or imitated languages. Seen from today's vantage point, I was taking part back then in a language in which I had nothing to express except a wish for more justice, and I was doing it because of my guilty conscience. I still have this wish, but I can't feel justified any more by using language considered progressive, in other words by expressing left-wing opinions. If I write a novel about the presence of the past in the present, then the novel expresses me all the more, the less I submit to the obtrusively present expectations of the *Zeitgeist* while I'm writing. Perhaps novels that do nothing but express the opinions required by the *Zeitgeist* don't even need to be written. Not even if they dispute the required opinion. They aren't actually narrative, but rather illustrative works. If I can participate in anything at all, it's only in publicly identifying defects in the removal of which I can participate. This applies to everything, up to the point of waging war. I can only endorse a war in which I would be prepared to participate. As a commander or as a combatant. Anyone who says there should be shooting must be able to push the button that releases the bombs. But I can't blame any intellectual who considers bombing necessary and, in sentences that dig deeply, proves first of all the necessity of bombing and then the historical sense of this manner of waging war. I even have to accept the fact that my inability to contribute an opinion favorable to war is harshly criticized.

After all, the spirit of the world appears first as the spirit of the age. And then it's called . . .

No, I avoid names. Whenever possible, even in conversation with myself. Hanspeter Müller, in his notes on St. Augustine's *Soliloquies,* wrote: "The ancients had the tendency, even when referring to a very specific author, of not introducing him by name but referring to him in a general allusion." And they were right, too, the ancients, because you really mean the thought, not the name. The nonsense about naming names is nothing but a journalistic tribunal. And the basic idea is: in what language am I best expressed? I could also have mentioned dreams, they too express us. But dreams, if one handles them consciously, lose even more than do conversations with oneself.

Every writer knows best up to what point he is contained or expressed in his language. I would no longer be contained in a language that places the executive office of capitalism under suspicion, or that recommends bombing, because I know from experience that after such a declaration of suspicion or a recommendation of war I would return to my novel, and in the language of the novel, which after all expresses what is inside me to a far greater extent, that suspicion and that bombing would not appear in the slightest. So I must be suspicious of my language when it is directed at an audience. It becomes a kind of stage language. The opposite of stage language is a conversation with oneself. Or so I hope.

2.

The clearer it is to me that no one will hear from me whatever is passing through my head, the more what is passing there is a conversation with myself. Even when this interior language is directed at or against one person or another. In a pure conversation with myself I don't need to be right, I don't need to prove anything, I don't need to make an effort to avoid misunderstandings. The ideal would be to speak in front of others as you do within yourself. But that will never be the case. You could dream of that: speaking in front of others, but not addressing them.

Avoid the tone of address. Anyway, logically there's no reason for someone to want to speak in front of others without wanting to address them. But what I have in mind is at least once to diminish the difference between the two languages, the language of internal conversation and the language of public address. Everyone knows this difference, I would hope. The internal conversation is a freer form of speech than the language of address. In an internal conversation you don't reach an opinion and then defend it more than is necessary against all other opinions. In the language of address it often happens that a critical opinion very quickly gains control over me. I must then mobilize everything that supports this critical opinion, and suppress everything that could undermine it. In the language of public address I reduce myself to sentences that sound as if I could be right. The more my sentences sound as if I want to be right, the further removed they are from the language to which I abandon myself in an internal conversation.

To suggest what I mean by citing two historical conditions of language: "Go ye therefore, and teach all nations. . . ."[3] That's a standard sentence of the language of address. The opposite: "Have you pray'd to-night, Desdemona?"[4] That's what concerns me: whether Desdemona prayed tonight or not. And the absurdity in the tragedy of Othello, namely that Desdemona was not at all involved with the other man. That doesn't interest me. That's of interest only outside, in the language of morality, of wanting-to-be-right, the language of founding or destroying states. What Iago says is true, even if it's a malicious lie a hundred times over. Othello's suffering makes the lie true. And Desdemona's death seals this truth. Othello's internal conversation is that of someone hopelessly in love. Whatever of this conversation makes its way into the outside produces a Iago and the intrigue that goes with him. This intrigue is theater in the simplest sense of the word. Melodrama. Naturally, my internal conversation, when it has once more arrived at the universalist standard statement "Go ye therefore and teach," presents me with its antithesis: "I know that I know nothing." But this sentence seems to me, even as I approach it, much too artificial. Addressed to the outside. While the sentence from Othello seems to me a voice from within. From within me. An expression rather than an insight. Existence rather than cognition. Essence instead of knowledge. I'm not sure if you could also say: suffering instead of acting. If it's about something political, yes you could. To suffer the cruelties of the war in Kosovo without placing yourself on the right side of the conflict by way of some opinion or other. And when it's about the German past, it's not very different. There's no chance of making yourself into a better person through righteous sentences, to serve the victims linguistically by casting convenient aspersions at the Germans, who either because of guilt or shame or even moral exhaustion can't do it themselves any more, or can't do it yet. These aspersions are extremely easy to cast. As long as you target others.

[3] Matthew 28:19.

[4] From Shakespeare, *Othello,* act 5, scene 2.

Never yourself. That's precisely it — the language of address. And I say this in a language that is entirely one of address. Dominated by the gesture of wanting-to-be-in-the-right. My internal conversation takes a different course. It does not stop at any point of agreement or contradiction. It goes through every conceivable possibility. It delves deeply into what is immoral or amoral, and thus also untenable. And it does this with every topic and circumstance. And it can wander and grope around for a long time in areas that are forbidden, or no longer authorized, until it once again reaches some points that may be appropriate for public consumption.

Socialization is the name we give to the process of educating people to become social beings. In a conversation with ourselves we experience the limits and shortcomings of our socialization. Socialization means being intellectually and spiritually housebroken. We're supposed to think nothing but what we can also express aloud.

The languages in which we address others are in the service of intentions, purposes, goals. They're applied languages. They can be very noble or very evil languages. But whether they're noble or evil, what they have in common is their goal-directedness. The posture of addressing others. Positivity. When I make use of these languages, I learn what I mean and what I want. And then I hope that I'm not merely what I mean and not merely what I want. I only want to *seem* as justified as the image I project of myself — I don't really want to *be* like that. In a conversation with yourself you are your own accomplice, even in the worst utterances. That is, you can easily be against yourself, since after all you know you're really for yourself. If you see a blatant reason to condemn yourself, then you represent the person who blatantly condemns himself.

I gave a speech in St. Paul's Church in Frankfurt that was discussed in public for some time afterward. Those who occupied my attention most were those who wrote that I should not have been permitted to say what I said in St. Paul's Church. I had evidently confused St. Paul's Church with the couch, they wrote. The reference was clearly to a psychoanalyst's couch. To judge from what I said there — it was also written — I belonged on the couch. Another wrote: he can think such things in private, but he can't say them in public. The people who reacted this way were leading intellectuals. In St. Paul's Church, one of the most public sites of all, one shouldn't say what one can think in private or say on the analyst's couch. I share this opinion. But what seems private and couch-like to my critics is to me my personal language. I know that I don't address my language as is the norm in such speeches, thus in the proper way. I also know that politicians and preachers address their speeches strictly. They calculate their effects. They want to have an effect on their audience. This stance is alien to me. I know, from my experience as a writer, that everyone reads his own novel when he reads one of my novels. I believe that anyone who listens to a speech understands it in his own fashion. I don't want to persuade him to understand the speech as I intend it. This is the freedom that prevails among people who do not see language merely as a tool for exchanging recipes. The way a person understands my speech or my novel is his responsibility, not mine. I was urged to call this or that reaction a misunderstanding. I had to decline. Everyone has the freedom to understand something as he must. It is not my job to prescribe a particular way of understanding. I also don't have to be in agreement with someone's way of understanding me. Every kind of understanding is a contribution to the whole. The politician speaks to achieve a particular effect. Must the writer submit to this usage of language? Then he must disguise himself. He must play the role of a politician, which, after all, he is not. One may expect of a politician that he act as he speaks. I, on the other hand, bear the hope that a writer may act in and through his speaking. But he can only do this if he remains within his own language. He can attempt to bring himself to speech as a contemporary in such a way that contemporaneity never becomes public in any of the usual languages of public address. A writer may be surprised that other writers say of him that it would have been all right to think in private what he said, but not to say it in public. I believe that a writer's only chance of contributing to a public discourse is to speak only of what is personal to him. It seems to me that it's not worthy of an intellectual to confuse the terms "private" and "personal." "Private" is that which requires discretion. "Personal" means my share of the whole, so in this case: my language. Nothing is less private than my language. My personal share in my language corresponds to my experience. But I don't want to pretend I don't know what was meant by the reproaches. It was about dealing with the German past. I wanted to speak publicly about what goes on inside me when I deal with this past. To speak publicly in front of others, but not to others. Thus precisely not in the officially implemented usage of language that is employed whenever this topic comes up, but rather in an unauthorized, so to speak unbaptized usage of language. This is a language stance that is not entirely different from that of a novelist; in any case, it's nearer to this than to the language of politicians, preachers, teachers, and journalists, which is used as a tool. It is the difference between language addressed to someone, and language that is involuntary. It seems to me that what is expressed by involuntary language might remind a listener or two of his own experience more than if he feels himself to be merely the target of an addressed language.

I hope that if you succeed in saying something important in an involuntary language, the listener may experience a kind of freedom. Freedom with respect to every form of dominant language usage. He doesn't have to adopt any of my ideas — in fact, he can't; he doesn't even have to believe anything I say; but he could, if he witnesses my involuntary use of language, share in the risk of using language in a way that has not always already been secured. He could be reminded, by the uncertainty or even anxiety in my language, or by my language's dependence on mood, of his own difficulty in finding an appropriate language for something so important. In this way a liveliness of exchange could arise, one that cannot arise from federal presidents and professors and the overwhelming non-ambiguity of their utterances. I admit, when I speak in this way I proceed on the assumption of a trust in language, in involuntary language, that I cannot presuppose on the part of all listeners. I do believe that virtually any form of literary writing derives its existence from this trust. My younger colleague Karl-Heinz Ott said recently: "Even in the driest treatise there lives a kind of music." I say: we search for the language in which we are most expressed. Then we could propose a kind of carat measurement: the carat count of a speech or of a language is determined by the extent to which the speaker or writer is contained in or expressed by his language. By this criterion, every speaker or writer would be expressed most of all by an internal conversation.

Conversation with oneself has after all been a literary genre for some time now. You could study what remains of the inwardness of a genuine, pure conversation with oneself in an involuntary, and then also in a voluntary, mode of address.

The *Soliloquies* of St. Augustine, the young city rhetorician in Milan, come more or less at the beginning of the European tradition of internal conversation, so I learn from my Latin scholar Fuhrmann. Even these display both forms: the internal conversation in itself, and the internal conversation for others. The internal conversation is a dialogue between "A" and "R": between Augustine and Ratio (Reason). To be sure, this is an addressed dialogue, for the Ratio that guides the conversation is energetically goal-oriented; but Augustine's Self is nevertheless still a genuine Self. This Self presents itself to us in the very opening section through a prayer that continues through several pages.

Addressed to God. And this is an addressee who does not patch up the Self with speech conventions, but rather one who — at least when the speaker's name is Augustine — opens up, rips open, provokes the

Self: ". . . I know nothing in the way that I wish to know God," says this Self. "But now I love nothing besides God and the soul, and I know nothing of either one." This comes across as an inward, perhaps even the most inward state. Augustine would like to believe, but everything required for this belief must first be given him by God; if God gives him what enables him to believe in God, then he can believe in God. "When I seek you, let me not encounter anything else in your place." In contrast to the Ratio, equipped as it was with all the philosophical refinements of his age, Augustine himself is pure inwardness, uncertainty, vehement poverty, and neediness. This is how a Self comports itself. To be sure, one that submits to a highly trained Ratio.

3.

So that I might be practical, here are two examples of my kind of internal conversation.

First internal conversation:

Our development has brought us to the point that we need not say or even write what we are thinking right away. Perhaps through this ability to be silent, the belief has arisen that we have a free will. After all, we don't always do what we want to do right away. Or we don't do it at all. But is a will that is denied thereby a free will? We have assessed a penalty for the ability to say something other than what we think. What is a lie and what is truth within ourselves is something we could also express through the difference between what is said and what is thought, or between what can be said and what cannot be said. We have become absolutely multilingual. We would have to declare it a speech convention that what we say need not be the same as what we think. What we say is what we want to say. That's something too, after all. What the morality that serves any kind of authority calls a lie arises entirely from inside ourselves. Corresponds to our momentary will. We would like to appear as we express ourselves at the moment, even if that's not what we're thinking or what we are at that moment. Maybe it'd even be alright with us if the image we're presenting of ourselves were indeed true. Maybe we present ourselves as better than we are. In any case: without the ability to appear different from what we are, we would be worse off. Fortunately, we can say something that we don't think. The moral grammar can coast on its own. Caesar non est supra grammaticos,[5] it was said once, when people had to protect their language from intimidation. Our languages

---

[5] Latin for "Caesar is not superior to the grammarians."

are more dependable than we ourselves are. In order to say something, we have to think it as well. Maybe we're not the way we say we are. But anyone who wants to can, if he examines carefully, determine at what point the illusion that we are capable of producing passes into being! Dependability would have to be newly defined. One must be able to depend on our untruths. If they should turn out to be friendlier than our truths, then it's a good thing one can rely on them. We have to stand by our untruths. Remain faithful to our lies. At least until the next opportunity to replace them with an even more favorable untruth. It may be some comfort that the negative potential of one syllable does not invalidate that main word: un-truth. After all, we do say flammable and inflammable,[6] so why not: truth and untruth. That's fitting.

Second internal conversation:

If I have wounded others exactly as often as they've wounded me, then everything is in order. Then this is a cosmos of pure harmony and justice. If I have wounded others exactly as often as they've wounded me, I must be a rather frightful person. Or else the world would be a maliciously conceived madhouse. Since that mustn't be assumed, I must have wounded others as often as they've wounded me. Everything's in order. It serves me right, or it would serve me right. Of course I'd like to maintain that once I was wounded more than I wounded others. And from this we can derive a cosmic principle: everyone was at one time wounded more than he wounded others. Everyone one time wounded others more than he was wounded. The world is founded on mistreatment. Through the veins of everything that lives flows this desire to wound. And the greater the desire to wound, the greater the prestige and power. And the greater the prestige and power, the greater the desire to wound. The attempt to arrive at a statement about quantitative comparison, one that would allow me to complain, is herewith retracted. Anyone who has ever wounded others has no basis to complain. This sounds harshly rigorous, or else noble, but it might be right. Anyone who has at any time wounded others must accept wounding from others. Wounding, but not necessarily those who wound. The ladies and gentlemen who feel so righteous just when they wound others remain a rabble faithful to the law of the world, a rabble to which one as a wounder of others naturally belongs oneself. I of course don't believe that the implicit self-reproach here really applies to me. I couldn't live if I had to think that even once I wounded others more than I was wounded. I hope that

---

[6] Walser uses the German words "Menge" and "Unmenge," both of which mean a large amount of something.

most people live in the hope that the world will one day ask their forgiveness. Those who don't know or don't need this hope are those who
wound in the course of performing their duty. It doesn't matter if I'm
one of them or not, but as long as they exist — of this I'm sure — there
will be wars.

4.

The train attendant stoops down to the travelers and offers service or
assistance of all kinds, and you can tell that she does not see the people
she wants to help. She obviously is completely focused on being helpful,
on serving. Her service is not in the slightest mechanical or thoughtless
or uninterested. Even though she knows none of her clientele personally,
her face beams with friendliness and warmth. She is a genius of devotion.
But since it is more than apparent that her devotion is not directed at
anyone personally but is rather pure devotion, it is devotion in and of
itself. Based on the wording, it seems paradoxical. In reality it's very
practical, very enjoyable, and even very beautiful. She whispers to me:
there exists a kind of devotion that is monologic, a kind of conversation
with oneself. She knows what she's doing; she probably senses the grati-
tude of her clientele. But she doesn't allow herself to be taken out of her
place and involved at the personal level. Whether she knows it or not: if
she looked at her people in such a way that she perceived their sweat and
their destiny, that would be the end of her useful beauty.

5.

And now in conclusion I abandon myself once more to the stance of
an internal conversation. Then someone, God knows who, whispers a
cue to me: if you have something to say, you don't need to contradict
anyone else. If you say what you have to say, you can sense its own limitations. You don't have to be right. Being right — that by itself turns
against someone else. To know better than someone else. As long as you
are subject to this gesture, you're avoiding your own task, your own
opportunity: to say what you have to say. I too have spent my life as a
writer in the charged atmosphere of having-to-be-right. And that has its
consequences.

   Why are poems the most beautiful specimens of language that we
know? Because the poem doesn't claim to be right. Why are politicians'
speeches the dullest linguistic specimens that we know? Precisely because
the politician is dependent on being right, or rather, creating the im-

pression that he's right. Participants in the sphere of public opinion know this compulsion. The most inhibiting form of being right is in the moral sphere. Having to create the impression that you're a better person than someone else.

You can defend almost anything that comes to your mind. If you have to. If you want to. But it's nicer to say the opposite of what you've just thought, or say something completely different, something that would never be expected in that moment. The more improbable, the more enjoyable. Have you pray'd to-night, Desdemona? Obeying an existential gravitation. But make sure that you don't accidentally raise another flag. You agree so little with yourself that you can only be perceived at all by people who do not agree with themselves either. For all upright, courageous, enlightened, wise, critical, serious, good people you don't even come into play if you're even halfway expressed by your language. If I wanted to promote something, it would be the joy of refuting yourself. Publicly. In parliament. In the newspaper. It should be a custom, it should be called a sign of culture, if someone who makes a statement also refutes what he just stated. He should present everything that comes into his mind in contradiction to what he has stated just as thoroughly as he did the statement. And please, no tongue-in-cheek[7] irony. If he then convinces us of the seriousness of his self-contradiction, and there's still something left from what he stated originally, then he has probably won us over to his position. In our current circumstances, it's too much to hope that this will ever happen. Nevertheless, you can still say it once.

To yourself.

I say to myself: no one is meaner than you.

And I add: that's rather comforting.

And I add to that: but also discomforting.

But not too much.

That's enough for today.

---

[7] Walser uses the English phrase.

Commentary

THIS ESSAY EXPANDS ON THEMES that were central to the 1998 Peace Prize speech: first, the opposition between the public and the personal sphere, and the languages associated with each, and second, closely related to the first, the contrast between literary language and language directed at some goal, which is often shaped by a particular ideology. The central concept of "Selbstgespräch" (a soliloquy or conversation where one is one's own audience) is clearly a somewhat defiant response to what he had recently experienced through and from the public sphere as a result of having tried, in his own view, to employ a more authentic form of expression in the Peace Prize speech and on other occasions.

He opens by contrasting spontaneous thoughts with those that one is compelled to think, either of one's own volition or by some external force. In the latter case, the language in which these thoughts get expressed is the standard language of the public sphere. Writers, he claims, if they are true to their craft, are "subject to and under the spell" of these thoughts and the involuntary language in which they are expressed. Their goal is not to control this language, but to allow themselves to be controlled by it. Referring to a comment made by a woman following one of his speeches that his literary works do not seem to reflect the left-wing ideology he had professed as a public spokesman, he reiterates the point made in the 1998 speech, namely that it is in his novels that he is really expressed. He hastens to add that he intends no criticism of those "journalists, politicians, or professors" who use language to express opinions, and use these opinions to distinguish themselves from others. But then, a few sentences later, after pointing out that neither a novel nor a drama should be used to express an opinion, he adds "neither should a speech or an essay." In other words, what might have been viewed at first as an invocation of the time-honored distinction in literary scholarship between literary and discursive language turns into a questioning of the very idea of discursive language — if a speech or an essay is not supposed to express an opinion, how, one might ask, does it differ from a poem or story?

Following on that comment, he says "I don't need to educate or enlighten anyone beside myself," and then proceeds to examine the notion of "Aufklärung" (enlightenment or education); whereas the English term "Enlightenment" still is used primarily to designate the historical epoch, in German it is commonly used to designate the goal or activity of the intelligentsia. The problem today, in Walser's eyes, is that this concept has come to mean "reproaching others for being insufficiently enlightened," or in other words being concerned above all to prove that one is right and others are wrong. He invokes Kant's famous definition of enlightenment to demonstrate that the term, properly understood, refers first and foremost to a process within oneself, thus not directed at others, and one that both presupposes and advances the cause of freedom. He then takes a swipe at "left-wing intellectuals" for utilizing the notion of enlightenment to validate their own concerns. Quoting a statement he made in 1972 regarding the contradiction between labor and capital, he is obviously owning up to the fact that he once was guilty of this as well, but then he adds "today I could no longer say that sentence." It is not that he has utterly renounced his past left-wing convictions; he simply feels now that they are "too abstract" and also motivated by his own guilty conscience. In this instance, he is referring not to guilt stemming from the German past but rather to what he characterizes as a state of dependence that is endemic to society and that, he claims, is the major source of social injustice. This notion of dependence, he argues, more accurately reflects the reality depicted in his novels, and thus the reality of his own perception, than do Marxist assertions about labor and capital.

He thus returns to the subject of the literary text, arguing once more that such a text can arise only when the writer abandons him- or herself to language: "meaning cannot be produced intentionally; it can only arise on its own." He goes on to emphasize the role of the reader in creating meaning, which he goes so far as to claim is "more a product of the reader than of the author." He will return to this theme a bit later when he refers to the reception of his 1998 speech.

He dwells again on the nature of language, which, he points out, is an element that unites people, but at the same time one that divides them, due to the diversity of languages created within any speech community — "Internal languages, external languages, adopted or imitated languages." He speaks of resisting the language that is forced on one from the outside, the "expectations of the *Zeitgeist*," adding that a novel that did nothing but fulfill these expectations could be dispensed with entirely. He then makes an interesting move, stating "If I can participate in anything at all, it's only in publicly identifying defects in the removal of which I can participate." In other words, he implicitly criticizes those who make pronouncements regarding domestic or international problems without having any intention of participating in the solution. He then refers implicitly to the NATO campaign in Kosovo, saying "I can only endorse a war in which I would be prepared to participate." There is an interesting ambiguity to this statement: does it amount simply to a formal abstention from taking any position regarding this military campaign, since he's not prepared to participate in it, or does it imply a critique of this military campaign? In the public view, his withholding of his endorsement of the bombing campaign (in contrast to other left-wing intellectuals such as Günter Grass) was regarded once again as evidence of his contrarian nature. In the essay, he does follow this statement with an assurance that he is not criticizing any intellectual who feels compelled to defend and justify the NATO campaign. But then he implies that a stance in favor of the bombing was in accord with the "Weltgeist," the spirit of the world, which he claims is the first manifestation of the *Zeitgeist,* which is then called — but he breaks off his statement at this moment, justifying this with his wish to avoid names. Here one cannot help but recall his avoidance of names in the 1998 speech, which was widely criticized for leaving the door open to an interpretation of his speech as criticizing Jewish Holocaust survivors and the families of victims who sought reparations from the German government. He quotes a classical scholar referring to Augustine's *Soliloquies* to support the practice of withholding names, claiming that what matters is the thought, not the person who expresses it. He concludes this section of the essay by repeating that he is suspicious of any use of language "directed at an audience," which is akin to stage language — the *Selbstgespräch* or conversation with himself is thus the antithesis of, and the antidote to, this kind of staged language.

But then the question arises: how is one supposed to speak with or to others? He says that ideally you should "speak in front of others as you do within yourself," but then adds right away that that will never happen. Still, he advocates that one avoid "the tone of address." The goal is the more modest one of diminishing the distance between public and personal language. The problem with public speech is that once you formulate an opinion, that opinion gains control over you and forces you to summon up all arguments in favor of it and suppress anything that speaks against it. He illustrates this distinction by juxtaposing Jesus' admonition in Matthew 28:19 "Go ye therefore, and teach all nations . . ." with Othello's question to Desdemona in act 5 of Shakespeare's play. It must be recalled that Othello is persuaded of the false accusation that Desdemona has been unfaithful to him, and he is about to kill her as a result of this. What is startling is that Walser regards Othello's question as the more authentic utterance, even though it is grounded in what is demonstrably false based on external reality. This reality, Walser asserts, is of no consequence; what matters is the inner truth of Othello's feelings. Evoking the authenticity he senses in Othello's words, he describes it in these words: "a voice from within. From within me. An expression rather than an insight. Existence rather than cognition. Essence instead of knowledge." But then he speculates that one might add to that "suffering instead of acting," and then says that that would apply to the political sphere, specifically the Kosovo conflict. The ideal then would be "to suffer the cruelties of the war in Kosovo, without placing yourself on the right side of the conflict by some opinion or other": in other words, to feel compassion for those affected by the conflict rather than to voice an opinion about the conflict.

But, not surprisingly, he takes this "political" opening to shift the topic to discussions of the German past, and ultimately to his 1998 speech and its reception. After speaking of the process of "socialization" as one in which one is trained not even to think anything that one would not be allowed to say aloud, he cites his own speech and aftermath as an example of "non-socialized" behavior. He calls particular attention to those voices who suggested he should not have been permitted to say the things he did, and that the fact that he did proves that he belongs on an analyst's couch — clearly the place where one may say those things that one is not supposed to say in public. But while acknowledging that there are things that should not be said in public, and that his language doesn't conform to prevalent norms, he insists on his right to his personal language. This language, in accordance with his prior remarks, is one that is not intended to persuade or achieve any goal. Further, it is the responsibility of the listener to interpret it as he or she will: "The way a person understands my speech or my novel is his responsibility, not mine." This is clearly a response to those who sought to mediate the debate by calling on Walser to clarify that he had not intended, for instance, a total suppression of public discussion of the Holocaust; but he was not willing to do so, for the reasons stated here.

At this point he makes a distinction to which he attaches considerable importance, between the terms "private" and "personal." Though one might comment that these terms (in both German and English) are often used interchangeably, he adopts the sarcastic tone that characterized portions of his speech and many of his statements during the public debate that followed when he says "It seems to me that it's not worthy of an intellectual to confuse the terms 'private' and 'personal.'" What is this distinction, and why is it so important to him? His explanation: "'Private' is that which requires discretion," in other words, it is that which should be voiced only on an analyst's couch. Thus Walser acknowledges that there are some ideas or kinds of language that are inappropriate for the public sphere. The term "personal," however, means "my share of the whole, so in this case: my language." This distinction is crucial for the understanding of the essay. One's language is at the same time what is most personal or distinctive about one, and what ties one most closely to the large community of which one is a member. It is in this sense that Walser wants the notion of a conversation with one's self to be understood: as an interior monologue that is intended for a wider audience, the members of which must interpret that monologue according to their own personal sensibility and language. And this illuminates how he envisioned his 1998 speech (whether this understanding is ex post facto or not would be hard to determine), namely as an internal conversation intended to be "overheard" by an audience that should be stimulated to its own reflections as a result. In speaking of "what goes on inside me" when he is confronted with images of the Holocaust, his hope is to allow his listeners to experience a kind of freedom, a reminder of their own difficulty in finding an appropriate language for the theme, and thus to generate a "liveliness of exchange" lacking in the discourse of politicians and professors.

He returns to elaborate further on the internal language he is talking about, citing Augustine once more, in particular the dialogues between Augustine's own self and "Ratio," the Reason that stands outside the self, and ultimately with God. He writes: "Augustine himself is pure inwardness, uncertainty, vehement poverty, and neediness. This is how a Self comports itself. To be sure, one that submits to a highly trained Ratio." By invoking Augustine, he affirms that there is indeed a reality outside the self to which the self is ultimately subject, but that this self can come to terms with that outside reality only by being true to itself.

In the remainder of the essay Walser offers some examples of what he regards as "conversations with oneself." The first deals with a reflection on whether or not to say what one is thinking, in light of external forces that determine what is acceptable. A person's awareness of these external constraints causes internal confusion between what is a lie and what is truth, especially since one's own thoughts and feelings are never constant. "Our languages," he suggests, "are more dependable than we ourselves are." And thus the apparently absurd conclusion is reached that we have to "remain faithful to our lies." In the second conversation, the subject is aggression among people. The speaker reflects on whether he has wounded others more than they have wounded him, and then tries to make sense of the situation — assuming a balance between wounding and being wounded, he first asserts this shows "a cosmos of pure harmony and justice," but then asserts that if this is the case, "I must be a rather frightful person." He ends this reflection by expressing the hope that people live in the hope that those who have wounded them will ask their forgiveness — as long as there are those who do not (he calls them "those who wound in the course of performing their duty"), he suggests, "there will be wars" — another reference to the Kosovo campaign. These two examples of "internal conversation" both show the fluid, back-and-forth quality that Walser sees as typifying internal conversation, and that forms a stark contrast to the one-dimensional, goal-oriented speech that characterizes the public sphere.

In the next section, he gives an example the relevance of which is not immediately apparent, namely the demeanor of a train attendant. What he emphasizes is the contrast between her focus on being helpful and serving others, and the warmth and friendliness she projects toward this end, and on the other hand, the fact that she knows nothing of the people she is serving and has no real personal connection with them. He calls this a kind of "monologic" devotion, but suggests that it is precisely on account of its monologic quality that she is able to serve others so well: "if she looked at her people in such a way that she perceived their sweat and their destiny, that would be the end of her useful beauty."

In the final section, Walser pleads for the possibility of vocalizing one's internal conversations, thus engaging in speech that does not feel the need to prove one is right and others are wrong, but simply to convey what goes on inside one, with all its internal contradictions.

*   *   *

In this essay Walser is both elaborating on the issues raised in his 1998 speech and defending the mode of speaking that he employed in that speech. One way of looking at his position is that he is advocating and employing a "literary" mode for public speaking; just as a novel or a poem should not be used to express an opinion, neither should an essay or public speech. This of course goes against the common assumption that most would make, namely that the former are "literary" modes, but that the latter are not and should employ language that is clear and unambiguous. Taken in a vacuum, Walser raises some interesting and arguably valid points — much public speech, particularly in the political sphere, does seem rather vacuous in its dogmatic certainty.

But Walser's speech did not occur in a vacuum — he was well aware of the expectations placed on him because of the occasion and the site, and he deliberately sought to challenge those expectations by adopting a different kind of language to address issues of Germany's relation to its past. Bubis ultimately withdrew the charge of "intellectual arson," by which we can understand him to have acknowledged that Walser was not seeking to give support to right-wing voices calling for an end to talk of the Holocaust. But if one can understand Walser's anger at those who call such voices typical of all Germans, it is still clear that he (at least in the speech) seems to deny that these voices are of any concern.

The essay reflects an ambivalence that can be seen throughout Walser's career. Speaking of his early career, Jörg Magenau writes:

> He viewed the public sphere as an expanded private space, in a sense as his living room. . . . Walser intervened constantly and diligently in the public sphere and at the same time defended the inviolability of the aesthetic. He claimed for himself the right to intervene in public debate as well as the right to retreat into the realm of poetry.[8]

There is no immediate problem if one chooses to make a speech and then withdraw into one's personal literary work; the problem arises, though, when the speech is heard as a public statement but is then claimed as a personal literary expression. The ambiguity is inherent in the very term "Selbstgespräch"; I have chosen not to translate it as "soliloquy," since this English word refers specifically to a stage monologue, and Walser at one point insists that his notion of "Selbstgespräch" is precisely an internal conversation that is not directed at an audience. And yet the German word clearly points to the notion of a staged soliloquy as one of its possible meanings, and thus this dimension cannot be dismissed as easily as Walser does when he calls the conversation with oneself "the opposite of stage language." Later he describes his goal as "to speak publicly in front of others, but not to others." But this might be seen as an accurate description of a dramatic soliloquy, so the distinction is not as clear as Walser earlier suggested. The problem is that it is crucial to his notion of "Selbstgespräch" that it be "overheard," and that it communicate with its listeners in an intense and personal fashion. But in this case, it is problematic to deny any responsibility for the impact one's speech has on the thoughts and feelings of its audience, and therein lies the essential problem with Walser's notion.

---

[8] Jörg Magenau, *Martin Walser: Eine Biographie* (Reinbek bei Hamburg: Rowohlt, 2005), 81.

Conclusion

IN 2002, FOUR YEARS AFTER the Peace Prize speech, Walser published his novel *Tod eines Kritikers* (Death of a Critic), which featured a corrupt and power-hungry literary critic and media celebrity named André Ehrl-König, who "happens to be" Jewish. Anyone familiar with the German literary scene would recognize Ehrl-König as a caricature of Marcel Reich-Ranicki. Even before the novel's appearance, it unleashed a scandal almost equal to the one following his 1998 speech: Frank Schirrmacher, the literary editor and co-publisher of the *FAZ*, who gave the introductory tribute to Walser prior to his speech in St. Paul's Church, and who was to defend him following the speech, announced in an open letter to Walser that he regarded the novel as a "document of hate" riddled with antisemitic clichés, and that therefore, contrary to their established procedure, there would be no advance publication of the novel in *FAZ*. The fact that one of Walser's prominent defenders now seemed to agree with his attackers not only reopened the wounds that had scarcely begun to heal from the Peace Prize debate, but in the eyes of many settled the issue once and for all — Walser had been found guilty of pursuing an antisemitic agenda. But even though few would claim that it was among Walser's better novels, many did defend it as fundamentally a satire and critique of the excessive power wielded by the mass media in the German literary industry. It was argued that for a writer to bear a grudge against Reich-Ranicki could hardly be regarded as proof of antisemitism, and that in fact Reich-Ranicki took advantage of his Jewishness to assume a particularly aggressive tone in his reviews, thus justifying the fictional reference to his Jewishness.

Three years later (2005), a young German scholar named Matthias N. Lorenz published his dissertation, in which he argued that, far from having changed his political orientation in the 1970s or 1980s, Walser had displayed antisemitic tendencies throughout his literary oeuvre, and in his speeches and essays as well.[1]

It is beyond the scope of this book to enter into the controversy regarding Walser's 2002 novel or his earlier novels and plays, but we may

[1] *"Auschwitz drängt uns auf einen Fleck": Judendarstellung und Auschwitzdiskurs bei Martin Walser* (Stuttgart and Weimar: J. B. Metzler, 2005).

consider the charge leveled by Lorenz and others on the basis of the essays and speeches presented here. Especially given the explosive nature of any charge of antisemitism leveled at a post-Holocaust German, such charges should not be made without conclusive evidence, and there is little in these texts to support this charge. What we have seen, as early as the 1965 essay "Our Auschwitz," is a strong sense that modern German identity is constituted in large part by the legacy of guilt for Nazi crimes, and thus that there is an unbridgeable gulf separating the descendents of the perpetrators from those of the victims. Matthias Lorenz points to Walser's problematic relationships with prominent German Jews of the past and present — the writers Heinrich Heine and Franz Kafka, the Nazi-era literary scholar Viktor Klemperer (in the publication of whose diaries Walser played a significant role), and contemporaries such as his long-time friend, the German literary scholar Ruth Klüger (she broke her ties with him following the publication of *Death of a Critic*), and of course the major public figures Marcel Reich-Ranicki and Ignatz Bubis. Given the public nature of his disputes with the latter two, it is perhaps more useful to consider Klemperer and Klüger and his relation to both. As to Klemperer, who died in 1960, Walser never met him, so what is significant is the role he played in the publication of Klemperer's diaries, and especially the way he presented Klemperer's life in his laudatory speech, a presentation that drew intense criticism (from Habermas among others) and which he defended in the Peace Prize speech. His insistence that the German-Jewish relationship not be viewed as one inevitably leading to the Holocaust is perfectly reasonable and unproblematic, in my view. What is more interesting is his obviously approving presentation of the Klemperer family's total assimilation: "an attempt, maintained over the course of fifty years, through baptism, marriage, and accomplishments to escape the lot of Eastern European Jews and become Germans, to assimilate completely." Thus one might surmise that a German-Jewish existence is affirmed when, and only when, it sheds all trace of Jewishness. In his friendship with Ruth Klüger (Walser is represented under the alias of "Christoph" in Klüger's memoir *weiter leben*[2]), Walser appeared at times to have displayed remarkable obliviousness to Klüger's Holocaust experiences — a lapse that anticipates his unbelievable comment to Bubis that he had dealt with the Holocaust while Bubis was pursuing his business interests. To say that Walser is subject to some complex internal conflicts in dealing with Jews in the past and the pres-

[2] The English version was published under the title *Still Alive* (New York: Feminist Press, 2001).

ent would seem obvious.[3] He has long been so preoccupied with the burden of German guilt that it seems difficult for him to feel, or at least to display, empathy for the victims. But to label this as antisemitism seems both inaccurate and counterproductive.

Walser's conflicts may also usefully be viewed as symptomatic of his generation of Germans. Male Germans born in the years 1926 to 1929 are sometimes referred to as the "Flakhelfer-Generation," the generation of Germans who were teenagers during the final months of the Second World War and who were recruited as anti-aircraft support helpers. Too young to bear any responsibility for Nazi crimes, they were nevertheless raised in a culture permeated with Nazi ideology, and to a greater or lesser extent they could not help but identify with their country and experience the German defeat as a catastrophe. Then, in light of postwar revelations regarding the Holocaust and other Nazi crimes, they clearly felt some guilt about this identification.

The psychoanalysts Alexander and Margarethe Mitscherlich explored the collective psyche of postwar Germans in their 1967 study *Die Unfähigkeit zu trauern* (*The Inability to Mourn*),[4] and argued that because of Germans' identification with Hitler, they were in a state of collective denial following the war, regarding both what had happened and their own responsibility for the crimes committed. In fact, there was a tendency to regard themselves as the victims — first of Hitler, then of the allied bombings and the rapes of German women by Soviet troops, and finally of the expulsion of ethnic Germans from Eastern Europe. The discourse of "Germans as victims" was generally carried out beneath the scrutiny of the world media, either in private conversations or among neo-Nazi and similar groups. One of the most significant features of Walser's 1998 speech is that it is one of the first instances of a respectable German publicly invoking the notion of Germans as victims — in this case, not so much during the war and the postwar period as during more recent times, when, according to Walser, unnamed outsiders wielding the "moral bludgeon" of Auschwitz are preventing Germans from assuming a "normal" identity. It is interesting to note that in the years since, a broader discourse of Germans as victims has opened up — Günter Grass's 2002 novel *Im Krebsgang* (*Crabwalk*, 2004) and W. G.

---

[3] Magenau, discussing the problematic representations of Jewish figures in Walser's early novels, writes: "As a German who stands burdened with guilt and shame in the wake of German history, he sees it as impossible to take a neutral stance towards Jews" (*Martin Walser: Eine Biographie* [Reinbek bei Hamburg: Rowohlt, 2005], 238).

[4] *The Inability to Mourn* (New York: Grove Press, 1975).

Sebald's 2001 essay volume *Luftkrieg und Literatur* (*On the Natural History of Destruction*, 2003) are two of the more prominent examples. It might be argued that this development represents a healthy turn — in contrast to the postwar tendency to focus only on German suffering, or to equate this suffering with the suffering inflicted by Germans and thus to "wipe the slate clean," this recent discourse neither denies the crimes of the Nazi regime nor equates German sufferings with those of Holocaust victims and others.

In Walser's case, the picture is a bit more clouded. On the one hand, Walser in the 1960s clearly stood apart from his generation and from the syndrome described by the Mitscherlichs, in his insistence on Holocaust remembrance and on the collective responsibility of Germans for what occurred. But, paradoxically, his particularly acute consciousness of the crimes committed by the German state leads ineluctably to an equally acute sense of the burden of guilt on German shoulders, which finally leads to resentment against those who (in his perception) use this guilt to keep him and other Germans in a perpetual state of shame and thus prevent him and them from attaining "normalcy." Walser, in keeping with his characteristically confrontational style, confronted his fellow Germans in the 1960s in their denial of guilt, and he confronts them in the 1990s, challenging what he calls the "lip service" of Holocaust remembrance. Despite this oppositional stance, in a broader sense one can view Walser as very much part of his generation of Germans, as he himself insisted in "Handshake with Ghosts" and elsewhere.

*   *   *

If one of the central themes of this volume has been the interplay of collective and personal identities, especially as they affect a German of Walser's generation, it might be appropriate for me to discuss my own collective identities, and how they might affect my perspective on Walser and the issues discussed here: as a Jew, as an academic in the field of German Studies, and as an American. My parents were Jewish refugees from Central Europe (Austria and Hungary) who came to the United States in 1939. My mother's father, about whom I heard a great deal in my childhood years, was a victim of the Holocaust. And yet both my parents were thoroughly assimilated Jews who had lost touch with almost all religious observance, but who were deeply immersed in German culture, and thus I inherited an essentially positive attitude toward most things German, in spite of my early knowledge of the Holocaust. My parents did make it clear to me that antisemitism was far from an exclusively German problem; my mother would mention that she had encountered far more antisemitism in her native Hungary than in her frequent visits to Germany (her eldest sister had married a German military officer from Munich in the 1920s). As I grew older and encountered Jews from less assimilated backgrounds, I realized that my relatively benign perspective on all things German was unusual for American Jews, many if not most of whom were prone to adopt the postwar stereotype of all Germans as Nazis.

My early work in German studies tended to avoid the difficult issues of the last seventy years, focusing primarily on turn-of-the-century and early-twentieth-century writers such as Rilke and Hofmannsthal. But partly as a result of the stronger sense of Jewish identity that I have developed as an adult, and also of my involvement in teaching on German-Jewish issues over the last ten years, I have become more and more involved with reflections on post-Holocaust German-Jewish relations, and my interest in Walser's texts has grown out of this new direction in my work. Without in any way compromising the judgments I have made regarding Walser, it is fair to point out that on the one hand I am aware of some problematic aspects of German attempts to deal with the past, and the ways in which these problems complicate the relations between Jewish and non-Jewish Germans, but on the other, I am also very aware that that past represents a huge burden for Germans, and that this must also be understood by those viewing the situation from the outside.

But if my identity as a Jew and as the grandson of a Holocaust victim predisposes me to empathize with the victims' collective rather than that of the perpetrators, my identity as an American opens up a different perspective. Lest I be misunderstood, it is not my intention here to equate the Holocaust with crimes of the American past — hundreds of years of slavery and the disenfranchisement of African-Americans for a hundred years following their "emancipation," or the slaughters of Native Americans in the nineteenth century. Nevertheless, it is still apparent that our country bears responsibility for enormous crimes against humanity, which were committed over a far longer period of time than the twelve-year Third Reich. I believe it is thus appropriate and helpful to reflect on how Americans deal with this legacy. Very few would suggest that Americans, or at any rate Americans of the last couple of generations, bear any direct guilt for slavery or segregation. And yet, it does seem that if Americans can and should feel pride in what their country has been and accomplished in the past and the present, then they must similarly accept responsibility for the more shameful chapters of this past. Though it would go far beyond the scope of the present work to survey how white Americans have coped, and are still coping today, with that legacy, one would no doubt find a great diversity of stances, ranging from total denial that these crimes of the past have any bearing on the present to an unhealthy obsession with this past guilt, one that makes it impossible to have an unburdened relationship with African-Americans. An example of this latter dilemma, one that bears striking similarity to the situation of Marcel Reich-Ranicki, is the reticence of many Americans in responding to some provocative African-American public figures such as Jesse Jackson or Al Sharpton. If one imagined a white American making statements such as those frequently made by Jackson or Sharpton, it seems obvious that they would provoke howls of protest, whereas Jackson and Sharpton go largely unanswered. What this illustrates is that the legacy of the past is one that continues to weigh on the collective shoulders of Americans, in a way that is not entirely unlike the situation of Germans sixty-five years after the Holocaust.

And yet in both societies one can point to hopeful signs that this dilemma may be alleviated, or even resolve itself, with time. In this light, a good deal of encouragement may be derived from comments that Walser made in an interview with the newspaper *Hamburger Abendblatt* in honor of his eightieth birthday in March 2007. In response to a question as to whether in retrospect he wished that he had given a different speech in 1998, he said no, but then added that he did regret his behavior following the speech. He specifically mentioned his conversation with Bubis, and said the following:

> I was so tense, so embittered, so pig-headed, that I responded to Bubis's offer to retract his accusation in a totally narrow-minded way. I should have held out my hands and thanked him for his conciliatory gesture. And then — this was worst of all — I wanted to brag and crow that I had been dealing with the German-Jewish problem longer than Bubis had. Seen from today, I regret this. It even causes me pain.[5]

A couple of months later, Walser was among the first visitors to a newly opened exhibition at the Frankfurt Jewish Museum in celebration of Bubis's life and legacy. The eighty-year-old Walser's ability to reflect on and acknowledge his short-sightedness thus may stand as a hopeful conclusion to this volume.

---

[5] *Hamburger Abendblatt,* Mar 16, 2007 (http://www.abendblatt.de/daten/2007/03/16/707285.html).

Suggestions for Further Reading

THE FOLLOWING IS A LIST of English texts relevant to the preceding volume: first, texts by Walser in English translation, and then some books on Walser's work, and finally texts dealing with how Germans, East and West, dealt and still deal with the Nazi past.

Texts by Martin Walser

The Gadarene Club. Trans. Eva Figes. London: Longmans, 1960.

Marriage in Phillipsburg. Norfolk, CT: New Directions, 1961.

Plays. Includes *The Rabbit Race* and *The Detour.* London: J. Calder, 1963.

The Unicorn. Trans. Barrie Ellis-Jones. London: Calder and Boyars, 1971.

Runaway Horse. Trans. Leila Vennevitz. New York: Holt, Rinehart & Winston, 1980.

Swan Villa. Trans. Leila Vennevitz. New York: Holt, Rinehart & Winston, 1982.

Inner Man. Trans. Leila Vennevitz. New York: Holt, Rinehart & Winston, 1985.

Letter to Lord Liszt. Trans. Leila Vennevitz. New York: Holt, Rinehart & Winston, 1985.

Breakers. Trans. Leila Vennevitz. New York: Holt, 1987.

No Man's Land. Trans. Leila Vennevitz. New York: Holt, 1989.

"A Runaway Horse" in *Three Contemporary German Novellas.* Ed. A. Leslie Willson. New York: Continuum, 2001.

Books about Walser

Martin Walser: International Perspectives. Ed. Jürgen E. Schlunk and Armand E. Singer. American University Studies. Series I, Germanic Languages and Literatures; vol. 64. New York: Peter Lang, 1987.

Oswald, Franz. *The Political Psychology of the White Collar Worker in Martin Walser's Novels: The Impact of Work Ideology on the Reception of Martin Walser's Novels, 1957–1978.* Frankfurt am Main; New York: P. Lang, 1998.

New Critical Perspectives on Martin Walser. Ed. Frank Pilipp. Columbia, SC: Camden House, 1994.

Pilipp, Frank. *The Novels of Martin Walser: A Critical Introduction.* Columbia, SC: Camden House, 1991.

Taberner, Stuart. *Distorted Reflections: The Public and Private Uses of the Author in the Work of Uwe Johnson, Günter Grass and Martin Walser, 1965–1975.* Amsterdamer Publikationen zur Sprache und Literatur, vol. 130. Amsterdam; Atlanta, GA: Rodopi, 1998.

Waine, Anthony Edward. *Martin Walser: The Development as Dramatist 1950–1970.* Bonn: Bouvier, 1978.

Texts Dealing with Germans and the Nazi Past

Fuchs, Anne, Mary Cosgrove, and Georg Grote, eds. *German Memory Contests: The Quest for Identity in Literature, Film, and Discourse since 1990.* Rochester, NY: Camden House, 2006.

Fulbrook, Mary. *German National Identity after the Holocaust.* Cambridge, UK: Polity Press, 1999.

Herf, Jeffrey. *Divided Memory: The Nazi Past in the Two Germanies.* Cambridge, MA: Harvard University Press, 1997.

Kattago, Siobhan. *Ambiguous Memory: The Nazi Past and German National Identity.* Westport, CT; London: Praeger, 2001.

Kramer, Jane. *The Politics of Memory: Looking for Germany in the New Germany.* New York: Random House, 1996.

Krondorfer, Björn. *Remembrance and Reconciliation: Encounters between Young Jews and Germans.* New Haven, CT: Yale University Press, 1995.

Maier, Charles S. *The Unmasterable Past: History, Holocaust, and German National Identity.* Cambridge, MA: Harvard UP, 1988.

Michman, Dan, ed. *Remembering the Holocaust in Germany, 1945–2000: German Strategies and Jewish Responses.* New York: Peter Lang, 2002.

Miller, Judith. *One, By One, By One: Facing the Holocaust.* New York: Simon and Schuster, 1990.

Mitscherlich, Alexander and Margarete. *The Inability to Mourn: Principles of Collective Behavior*. Trans. Beverly R. Placzek. New York: Grove Press, 1975.

Neumann, Klaus. *Shifting Memories: The Nazi Past in the New Germany*. Ann Arbor: U of Michigan P, 2000.

Niven, Bill. *Facing the Nazi Past: United Germany and the Legacy of the Third Reich*. Oxford; New York: Routledge, 2001.

Schlant, Ernestine. *The Language of Silence: West German Literature and the Holocaust*. New York: Routledge, 1999.

Sontheimer, Michael. "Why Germans Can Never Escape Hitler's Shadow." *Spiegel Online*, http://www.spiegel.de/international/0,1518,345720,00 .htm.

Taberner, Stuart, and Paul Cooke, eds. *German Culture, Politics, and Literature into the Twenty-First Century: Beyond Normalization*. Rochester, NY: Camden House, 2006.

Taberner, Stuart, and Frank Finlay, eds. *Recasting German Identity: Culture, Politics, and Literature in the Berlin Republic*. Rochester, NY: Camden House, 2002.

Weissmark, Mona Sue. *Justice Matters: Legacies of the Holocaust and World War II*. Oxford, UK: Oxford University Press, 2004.

Index